Published by Kegedonce Press
11 Park Road, Cape Croker Reserve
R. R. 5, Wiarton, Ontario, N0H 2T0
www.kegedonce.com

Administration Office/Book Orders
RR#7 Owen Sound, ON N4K 6V5

Design: Red Willow Designs (http://www.redwillowdesigns.ca)
Printed in Canada by: Gilmore Printing Services
Printed on: Supreme Matte
Text set in Electra

All rights reserved.
No part of this book may be reproduced in any form or by any electronic or mechanical means including information storage and retrieval systems, without permission in writing from the Publisher. Member of Access Copyright

Sales and Distribution - http://www.lpg.ca/
LitDistco:

For Customer Service/Orders
Tel 1-800-591-6250 Fax 1-800-591-6251
100 Armstrong Ave. Georgetown, ON L7G 5S4
Email orders@litdistco.ca

Library and Archives Canada Cataloguing in Publication

Johnston, Basil, 1929-
 Think Indian : languages are beyond price / Basil Johnston.

ISBN 978-0-9784998-7-7

 1. Indians of North America--Languages--Social aspects. 2. Indians of North America--Ethnic identity. 3. Indians of North America--Intellectual life. I. Title.
 E98.E85J63 2010   306.44089'97   C2010-906710-X

Kegedonce Press gratefully acknowledges the generous support of:

ONTARIO ARTS COUNCIL
CONSEIL DES ARTS DE L'ONTARIO

We acknowledge the support of the Canada Council for the Arts which last year invested $20.1 million in writing and publishing throughout Canada.

Canada Council   Conseil des Arts
for the Arts   du Canada

Praise for TH!NK INDIAN

Think Indian: Languages are Beyond Price, Basil Johnston, Kegedonce Press, 2011
"Basil Johnston has long been one of my favorite writers. His is always a unique and truly indigenous voice whether his focus is on storytelling or the sacred, the history and culture of his own nation or his inspiring personal journey out of the labyrinth of the Indian boarding schools into prominence as an internationally known author.

I always expect the best from Basil, but this new book exceeds my expectations. THINK INDIAN is at once amusing and thought-provoking, a fine blend of scholarship and storytelling. These well-crafted essays -- ranging explorations of the importance of Native languages and prescription for their preservation to personal musings on the ironic positions in which modern Native people find themselves --
are a pure delight."

- Joseph Bruchac, author of the best selling *Keepers of the Earth: Native American Stories and Environmental Activities for Children* from his *"Keepers"* series

Praise for *Gift of the Stars*

Gift of the Stars, Basil Johnston, Kegedonce Press, 2010
"While also serving as a mantra for the study of the Ojibwe language, *(The Gift of the Stars)* advances the knowledge so necessary for Ojibwe students today. There is a critical need for academic materials to revitalize the language in a time when it does face ultimate extinction. Basil's work goes a long way to stemming the tide."

— Dr. Cecil King, founder of the Indian Teacher Education Program, University of Saskatchewan and Professor Emeritus, Queen's University

Praise for *Honour Earth Mother*

Honour Earth Mother, Basil Johnston, Kegedonce Press, 2003
"Basil Johnston writes of the real world at a time when reality seems to be disappearing from our vision. He knows what his ancestors have always known, that the only way to live on earth is to be a part of it. His new book is a remarkable examination of the connection of human beings to the Earth Mother. I heartily recommend it."

- Farley Mowat

"In *Honour Earth Mother*, Johnston explores the sacred, the creation, and the mystery from a Native American point of view. The result is an intriguing contribution to the environmental studies and the literature of place."

- *News From Indian Country*

TH!NK INDIAN

LANGUAGES ARE BEYOND PRICE

BASIL H. JOHNSTON, O.ONT., LLD., B.A.

© 2011

TH!NK INDIAN

– CONTENTS –

THINK INDIAN PREFACE	i
INTRODUCTION	1
OUR ANCESTRY IS OF THE SKY	6
I'M GLAD GOD IS NOT PERFECT	15
WHAT'S YOUR DIALECT?	24
HOW DO WE LEARN LANGUAGE? WHAT DO WE LEARN?	34
HOW SHOULD OJIBWAY OR OTHER TRIBAL NAMES BE SPELLED?	45
DO SOMETHING FOR YOUR PEOPLE	55
COWBOYS AND INDIANS	63
IS THAT ALL THERE IS? TRIBAL LITERATURE	73
ONE GENERATION FROM EXTINCTION	86
THE LAND WE CANNOT GIVE	94
PREFACE TO "DANCING WITH A GHOST"	100
THE MODERN WEENDIGOES	110
IRON RAY	115

TH!NK INDIAN

– CONTENTS –

Walter "Chick" Johnston	120
Languages Are Beyond Price	125
"They Didn't Teach Us Anything"	133
I Always Wanted To Be An Indian	144
You Can't Tell Stories In The Summer	153
Indian Identity — Who Are We?	159
Kitchi-Manitou Has Given Us A Different Understanding	168
Think Indian	177
Looking Back. From Writing To Publication	190
Tom Didn't Fail! He Succeeded	199
No Man Begins To Be Until He Has Received His Vision	203
Skills Or Understanding, Knowledge Or Wisdom	213
Where Is The Flour?	221
Is There A Place For Me On This Blanket?	229

TH!NK INDIAN
— Preface —

This series of articles should be seen as an outcry against Ministries of Education, Indian Affairs, universities, museums, seminaries, that bear a direct or indirect influence upon the education of teachers, professors, anthropologists, authors, publishers who have presented our ancestors as superstitious primitives whose only interest were their bellies, shelters and how to get from here to there, summer and winter. In their preoccupation with the here and now, primitives could not possibly grasp the notions of values, rights, duties, freedom, government, institutions, and matters of the intellect that only the civilized and Christian can conceive and exercise.

As part of their training, universities sent their budding anthropologists, archaeologists, ethnologists out on field trips to gather information and submit their reports. None of the students was required to learn the language of the people that he was studying.

Without language the student could not get into the heart, mind and spirit of his subjects, into their inner world. Outside would he ever remain, trying to look in from their physical world.

On graduation these newly minted scholars will teach in universities, colleges, museums, serve as consultants to the Ministries of Education, publishing houses, authors, Indian Affairs and serve as expert witnesses in the courts. There in these forums these experts will discuss and argue what they know about the physical culture of the Natives, nothing of their values, beliefs, institutions, outlooks.

In my community of Cape Croker all but a handful of speakers will be buried, along with the language. After them there will be no more language, nothing to distinguish the residents of this reserve from their neighbours.

THINK INDIAN

A good part of the decline in the vitality of our language may be set to our own people's indifference. They don't want or care for their heritage, their identity.

We've had language instruction in our community school for over 20 years, but none of our students can be said to speak the language. They may know a few words and phrases, but to carry on a conversation … no!

To listen to our language teachers and to glance over the curriculum issued by the Ministry of Education, the linguistic is evident. Students play sex games with the gender of words. "Is it animate or inanimate?"

A year or two at teachers' college and a year or two more in a primary or secondary school would have taught consultants something about the art of teaching.

For the extra burdens that Native students have to bear in learning their ancestral language, the Ministries of Education are to blame. Native children are required to speak, read, write and master a new phonetic system, all at the same time. Before English or French speaking youngsters are allowed to pick up a pen to learn to print, they have had at least six years of speaking their language. They are now ready to learn phonics and become literate.

And what is it that our youth are deprived of without knowledge of their ancestral language? Seven or eight years ago I asked high school youngsters from Kettle Point and Sarnia why they had taken an Anishinaubae language course. At the finish of the weekend seminar a grade 12 student told me in answer to my question that she had taken language studies to learn who she was. She understood that language is the key to self knowledge.

TH!NK IND IAN
— INTRODUCTION—

THINK INDIAN!
THINK! INDIAN!

Away back in the 1970s I was invited to the University of Saskatchewan to deliver lectures and talks to faculty and students. I regarded the invitation as a singular honour that demanded the best I could deliver and measuring up to the distinction of addressing scholars and academics of eminence. I set to work preparing my lectures. I would make my mark. The audience would remember my words and remarks and want to hear more.

To make the impression upon the academic community I decided to imitate some of the members of the Learned Society that I had heard and seen at one of the universities in Southern Ontario, which one I cannot recall, who read their presentations from notes and written texts. That was the way it was done and that was the way I was going to do it.

When I finished writing the texts of my lectures, I rehearsed the deliveries so that I would sound sincere, profound. On the flight to Saskatoon I read and re-read my presentations. I wasn't going to flub a word or a line.

On the morning of my first lecture I was ushered with considerable pomp and ceremony through the aisle of the auditorium and on stage. Already there was a large crowd. From where I sat on stage it looked as if every seat was occupied, but that is hard to say in the face of the stage lights that shone directly into my eyes, preventing me seeing into the dark gloom.

Finally, after many introductory remarks about my career and achievements, I was introduced.

To the lectern I went with my notes in a filing folder in hand. "Ladies and Gentlemen," said I. "I'm delighted to be here with you this morning, delighted to have been invited by my friend Dr. Art Blue; delighted to have accepted your invitation." Then I opened my folder, began reading.

Within five minutes I had lost my audience. I knew it. I could feel it. I could sense it. I felt that many in the audience wanted to slip out but could not. They were trapped. I wanted to do something, say something that would draw the audience back to me and my message that I so wanted to impart. But I was trapped. My text would not let me go. I could not stray from it. I had to cling to it to the end. Time took hold of me, held me back; it would not hurry to put an end to my agony. I read on.

At last my longest hour of agony was over. As quickly as I could, I retreated to my room to hide and to brood. I felt bad for Dr. Blue, for Cecil King. I felt bad for my fellow North American Indians. I had let them down. I felt bad for me, ashamed, embarrassed.

I looked at my filing folders, thought of all the hours of work that had gone into the preparation of the texts that they contained. With heartache and misgiving I tore up my notes and pitched them in the wastebasket.

Next day there were 15, maybe 25, in the auditorium. I told them what stories I knew. I wish that I could say that I won the audience back in large numbers, but I did not. I botched up my first speaking engagement.

From this experience I learned that the written word is meant for the eye, the spoken word intended for the ear.

For some time afterwards I wrote down my presentations, mastered them and delivered them as if my remarks were off the cuff. But more and more I was telling stories that would explain themselves.

THINK INDIAN

The title for this manuscript came from Thunder Bay where I was to give the keynote address to the teachers teaching in the remote regions in Northwestern Ontario.

After I checked into the hotel and registered with the association organizing the event, I went to my room, to study my notes for my address the following morning. Around mid afternoon I received a call from one of the organizers. "Would you mind giving the after-dinner address this evening?" the voice asked.

I hemmed and hawed pleading, "This – I'm not prepared; this isn't part of the agreement…" The voice cut in, "I know. But our after-dinner speaker can't make it … it's a family emergency.… Can't you help out? We'll pay you what we had set aside for the after-dinner speaker."

All doubts were removed.

As after-dinner speaker I sat near the front with a group of principals. I found it difficult to eat, think about what I was going to say and to listen and take part in their discussion of 'new math' and the merits of 'sight reading' as opposed to learning phonics first. From shop talk the discussion drifted to the previous year's event and the remarks made by the keynote speaker. Point by point the principal dissected the presentation delivered by the previous year's speaker. By the time that the principals had done re-hashing last year's keynote address, my speech was demolished. The previous speaker had covered the points that I had intended to tell. "Same old Southern Ontario solutions to Northern Ontario!" they snorted. I had no speech. I had to start over.

Right after my after-dinner address, I caught a cab and went back to my hotel room to put something together for tomorrow's offering. Instead I went to sleep, tired, … no, procrastinating.

At 5:00 AM I woke up. After shaving and showering I paced the corridors and the streets seeking inspiration but finding none. What do you say to teachers in Northwestern Ontario that would be relevant to the learning needs of their students in remote, isolated communities? I had no solutions to offer teachers that would help them prepare their students for life in the outside world and the life of technology and profit, wealth and cars.

Back in my room I picked up my pen to set down whatever stray thoughts that might wander into my mind, but before I could jot down a single idea, the phone rang.

THINK INDIAN

The caller introduced himself as Gerry, whose last name I cannot now recall but it was French, a consultant with the Ministry of Education. He wanted to talk to me, right now; the matter couldn't be put off. He was coming over right that moment. He spoke in my language; that is what disarmed me.

What we discussed I cannot recollect. My mind was on the presentation that I was to give at 9:30. I had to be there by 9:00 to meet my hosts. I hadn't the faintest idea of what I was going to talk about.

"I guess I'd better be on my way" I said, after looking at my watch.

"I'll drive you there," my guest offered.

On the way to the university a car, mufflerless, roared by us. Attached to its bumper was a wide band sticker bearing the words "THINK INDIAN". I jotted them down on a piece of paper.

At Lakehead University I was conducted into the foyer adjoining the university auditorium. There I met Jim Witcher, Superintendent of Education for the Northwest region of Ontario. Originally Jim Witcher was from Colpoys Bay, about 12 miles from Cape Croker, my home. Besides Mr. Witcher there were others in the foyer. "Think Indian! Think Indian!" swam through my mind.

"How much time do I have?" I asked Jim Witcher, with a wish that he'd say "30 minutes". Instead he said, "Two hours." How was I going to talk for two hours on 'Think Indian'?

Jim got up; spoke about my qualifications that might convince teachers that what I had to say might be worth listening to … "I now introduce Mr. Basil Johnston."

After I finally got the grumpiest teacher to allow a smile (teachers and professors are among the hardest of the hard to put into a receptive mood), I paused before commanding them to "THINK INDIAN", pausing once more to let the words sink in. Then I began. The ideas flowed into my head, words poured out of my mouth. They spilled out until Jim Witcher nudged me. I had spoken for two hours.

Later, during coffee, several people asked me for a text of my remarks. I didn't have any. But it was gratifying to receive some invitations to deliver the same address to teacher gatherings in Southern Ontario. In preparation for these events I wrote "Think Indian," herein included from what I remembered of my remarks in Thunder Bay.

THINK! INDIAN!

I was selling books in Sault Sainte Marie, Ontario some years ago at the Ramada Inn. Two big burly Indians, both about 6'4", making them appear burlier, came by my table. They stopped. One of the men, an Anishinaubae from Northern Michigan wearing a white shirt, giggled, pointed out the manuscript to his companion and then read the title aloud, emphasizing "THINK! … INDIAN!" Then he and his companion broke into thunderous laughs.

There you have the origin of the articles in this collection and source of the titles.

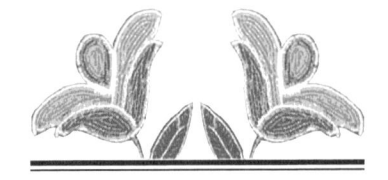

OUR ANCESTRY IS OF THE SKY

OUR WELL-BEING IS OF THE SKY

OUR DESTINY IS IN THE SKY

BASIL H. JOHNSTON, O.ONT., LLD., B.A. © SEPT. 5, 1983

OUR ANCESTRY IS OF THE SKY

Before humankind, there were only sky-beings, unknown and unnamed, who inhabited space. One of these sky-beings, Geezhigoquae (Sky-woman), gave birth to twin beings who destroyed one another before they and their kind could propagate the earth. It was at this time that the earth itself flooded, with only the water-beings surviving; the trout, the whitefish, the sturgeon and their kind; the beaver, the muskrat, the fisher and their kindred; the loon, the duck, the goose and other species of their genus. It was while the earth was under water that Geezhigoquae conceived a second time and gave birth to our ancestors, the Anishinaubaek (the Good Beings) on Michillimackinac, an island formed from a morsel of soil upon the back of a turtle.

After the first children grew into adulthood, able to care for themselves, Geezhigoquae returned to her abode in the skies and, as a reminder of her motherhood, placed the moon in the sky. Men and women are to recall their genesis and honour woman-kind whenever they see the moon.

The Father of the Anishinaubaek, symbolized by the sun, resides too in the sky.

We are the off-spring of manitous, best translated as the "mysteries."

OUR WELL-BEING IS OF THE SKY

As our origin is of the manitous of the sky, so we owe our well-being to the good will of the manitous who abide in space.

In the beginning and for untold generations thereafter, men and women flourished, living without ever having to suffer from want or pain, until a man challenged a manitou of the underworld to a test of powers with life or death at stake. The manitou of the underworld overcame the man and might have destroyed him entirely had not man besought the manitous of the sky for aid, and got it. But the good life that the Anishinaubaek had heretofore been accustomed to came to an end. Very different was life from that time on; the seasons were unbalanced, the days unsettled; humankind's health was no longer firm, and his life was cut short; the abundance that once was certain was no longer assured; and his spirit, never before troubled, was now open to bad dreams. The good life was no more.

THINK INDIAN

From time to the present men and women turned to the sky, not only in remembrance of their origin but also in seeking the good will of the manitous in their lives and in all their undertakings of whatever nature.

Out of an abiding reverence and sense of thanksgiving grew the practice of offering thoughts or prayers in the morning and again in the evening to Kitchi-Manitou, The Great Mystery. In the mornings when the Anishinaubae faced the east, he saw in the dawn the renewal of life and strength and the regeneration of the tribe, while in the setting of the sun he perceived wisdom and old age and finally death. The very wax and ebb of day served as a daily reminder to the Anishinaubaek of the cycle of life, ever to be respected and cherished.

The daily rise and wane of sun represents the human experience of life and death as it does a cosmic struggle. One medicine man, according to story, challenged another to a contest of powers. The first caused the sun to stop in its orbit in the middle of the sky so that it would ever be day and that humankind would ever be young. The people rejoiced but at last they grew weary of the mid-day sun and of youth; they turned to the second medicine man who set the sun once more in motion, restoring night, old age and death to their proper place in the natural order of being in the physical world.

Now just as there is the daily rise and set of sun giving day and night, so is there the annual change of season, giving summer and winter, a period of growth and decline. What we now know of it was not always so. Both Abi-boon (Winter) and Neebin (Summer), coveting the year, made war upon each other for primacy over and possession of the entire year. The Anishinaubaek endured so much misery during the struggle that the enemies were finally persuaded to a truce by which the year was partitioned equally between them.

But before the division of the year into summer and winter was settled once and for all, Abi-boon took Neebin prisoner and locked him up somewhere in the skies. It was the fisher who, learning of the act and where Neebin was concealed, set out to free the prisoner. Now while he managed to set Neebin free, Fisher himself was caught fast, his trailing tail fused to a rift in the sky that had clapped shut as Fisher made his way out. His image has ever remained transfixed against the sky as the Fisher with a Broken Tail (The Big Dipper).

Until these events in the sky took place the Anishinaubaek casually honoured Kitchi-Manitou and Muzukummaki-quae (Mother Earth) in private petitions, but after these happenings, they venerated in a more formal way in the ritual of the Smoking of the Pipe of Peace, not only Kitchi-Manitou and Muzukummaki-quae but also the manitous who presided over the four cardinal points and governed the seasons and, indirectly, man's life.

By offering the incense of tobacco, the Anishinaubaek sought not only to appease the manitous who exercised dominion over night and day, summer and winter, but also guidance in the conduct of their lives and affairs for every daily or seasonal change that occurred in the world around above, influenced their lives for better or for worse, the better being fair weather and abundance and the worse being tornadoes, blizzards, drought, killing frosts, which they regarded as forms of benefaction bestowed or retribution exacted for the moral character of their acts.

What they knew and understood of human nature the Anishinaubaek expressed in terms of the warmth of summer and cold of winter, which brought either benefit and good will or harm and ill will. During the Smoking of the Sacred Pipe, tribal leaders asked Neebin to instill in them the spirit of generosity and wisdom so as to render decisions that would do the most good.

Since death was instituted, the forebears of the Anishinaubaek also abide in the sky, the Land of Peace. They too, no less than the manitous, deserve remembrance and, when they are neglected, reproach the living for their neglect with thunders and lightnings. Another legend relates that it is the Thunder Birds who cause the thunders and lightnings in revenge for having once been driven into the sky from their mountain home. It was to appease and propitiate the grandfathers and grandmothers or the Thunder Birds that the custom of offering tobacco during a thunderstorm was started.

But fortunately we have foreknowledge of coming storms. Like watchful parents, Father Sun and Grandmother Moon give humankind warning by donning a parhelion one, two, and sometimes three days before a storm.

Now what of the stars? Originally they were not there; there was nothing except the sun and the moon. Generations passed before the Fisher stars were transfixed in the skies. Other than the sun, the moon and the Fisher stars, the sky was void, and might have remained so had not a young Anishinaubae fallen in love with, captured and then married a sky woman who, along with her sisters, used to descend from the sky in a craft to play with little animals in a meadow near the young man's home. And, even though she bore a son, the sky-woman was ever unhappy, longing to be with her own kind and kin. Then one day she remembered the chant that used to transport her and her sisters from their abode in the sky to earth and back again. She constructed a craft and chanted her song. At once she and her son were borne to her home in the sky where she was re-united with her parents.

After long separation the son, now a young man, was allowed to go to earth to visit his father whom he longed to see. On his return to the sky the son asked that his father be brought to their home. The boy's grandfather agreed on condition that the earth being bring sacks of brightly coloured pebbles. When the grandfather received the offering of brightly coloured pebbles, he cast them into space where at once they became bright glittering stars. And like the sun and moon, the stars change their hues and frequency of light to give humankind foreknowledge of the weather to come in the seasons immediately ahead.

By their very distance and beauty, within vision yet beyond reach, stars have ever held the fascination of humankind in much the same way as ideals move men and women to aspirations which they may never attain but which will nevertheless make them the better for their efforts.

Only in striving for ideals will men and women derive good in themselves and confer a benefit upon humankind. As an example, a young man fell in love with a star whom he lured to earth with promises. In coming to join her lover, the star fell into waters where she was instantly transformed into a water lily which multiplied at once into countless flowers of immense beauty.

As men strive for ideals, so they sometimes pursue ends of a very different character. Two young women asked one another as they looked skyward one evening which of the stars they would choose in marriage. One chose the brightest red star (Mars) while the other the brightest white star (Venus?). While they were asleep both young women were transported into the sky where they woke to find men at their sides; the young woman who had chosen the red star found a young man beside her, and she who had longed for the white star an old, old man. There in the sky the young women remained against their wishes until an old woman set them free by letting them down to earth on a rope through a hole in the sky that she had made.

And it is ever so with the Anishinaubae to let his mind leave his head and the present to wander among the stars and beyond. But it is not only his mind that is disposed to roam the heavens and other dimensions of time; his spirit has even greater predilection to enter the world of spirits and manitous who reside in the skies and to find therewith inspiration.

During a vision quest a young man's spirit was taken into the skies, directly to the abode of the Autissokaunuk (Muses), the patrons of music and of echoes and of prophecies.

There, in the presence of the Autissokaunuk, he intoned a chant of petition in the language of the patrons, not his own but a gift of the manitous:

> *N'daebaub auzhiwi-anungoong,*
>
> *K'gah kikinowaezhigook anungook.*
>
> *I can see to the other side of the stars,*
>
> *The stars will guide you.*
>
> *N'daebitum auzhiwi-anungoong,*
>
> *K'gah noondaugook anungook.*
>
> *I can hear the other side of the stars,*
>
> *The stars will hear you.*
>
> *Kaugigae n'gah daebitaugoos.*
>
> *Timeless is my voice.*

K'gah waussae/aubindum nebau/in,

K'gah gawaek-oshae nebau/in.

Even in sleep you will perceive,

In sleep you will hear.

Ae-naubindumun dah izho-waebut,

K'zhawaenimik Kitchi-Manitou.

What you dream will be,

The Great Mystery is generous with you.

Maukinauk k'gah mizhinawae/ik,

Tchi mino-dodomun, k'bawaudjigae.

Through the turtle will you speak,

For good will you dream.

Nindo-waewaemishinaung.

Call us.

    The Autissokaunuk too sang to him, for it was they who had summoned him to the skies and, by chanting to him, gave him their language. They then returned him to earth. As the manitous, for that is what the Autissokaunuk are, summoned him to their presence, so the young man could, with the language conferred upon him, summon the manitous for their help and guidance on behalf of the people.

Even in sleep a man or a woman's spirit ventures into space by means of dream, beholding visions and, at times, revelation that needs to be fulfilled. To seek answer or revelation and to receive one or the other through dream is a unique power or mystery that few possess. Medicine men and women are endowed with such, as are Namers of children.

From the moment that Cheengwun's spirit left his being to pass into the world of manitous in the sky to do battle with and to overcome a monster who was destroying children, he became a "namer." All such talents or powers that medicine men and women possess and exercise have their origin in the sky, bestowed by the manitous.

All the manitous of the sky had their origin in space except for one. Pauguk was a man who coveted his brother's wife and, in order to gain her, killed his own brother by drowning him. For his crime the tribe banished Pauguk from the village.

Pauguk left by canoe and, as he crossed a lake, was swamped by a sudden storm and drowned; his body later washed up on a rocky shore where his corpse was wedged between rocks. His soul/spirit called out for "help," for how long no one knows until at last a man and a woman heard the call and set Pauguk free. At once the skeleton, all that remained of Pauguk, flew into the sky at a point midway between the sun and earth, destined ever to be driven by winds around the earth, to nearly be set afire by the flames of the sun in summer or to be wracked by the freeze of ice in winter. Pauguk, once man and earth being, an exile, now a sky-being, still calls out from the heights for amnesty, by moan in summer night and the rattle of bone in winter.

OUR DESTINY IS IN THE SKY

Our origin is in the sky; so is our destiny. Somewhere in the vast space at the very end of the Path of Souls (The Milky Way), which extends to the other side of the stars, is The Land of Peace, humankind's final destiny.

We know this because some men and women have been there, and it is from them that we have come to know something of the nature and character of the life after.

Those who have been there say that the passage from this life on earth to the Land of Peace takes four days, and that along the Path of Souls are numerous tests and intense cold, similar to those that beset men and women in this life whose only purpose is to assess the worth of the soul/spirit, now become a shade.

To provide the deceased with the means to hunt along the way, the mourners buried a bow and arrows, flint, pipe and tobacco, a medicine bag, and a bowl and spoon; and to keep the soul/spirit warm during the journey the mourners kept a fire burning on the burial mound for four days whose reflection can be seen on certain evenings in the northern skies (Aurora Borealis), and for the entire four day watch a member of the Medaewaewin counselled the soul/spirit about the way of life in order to strengthen him.

At the end of the four day journey the soul/spirit will come to the Land of Peace whose form is much like the land that we are familiar with but in substance incorporeal, where either he or she will be welcomed with a festival by all kin. The days thereafter will be spent in hunting, fishing and berry-picking, and in the celebration of festivals as a continuation of existence, only in a different mode.

When the Anishinaubaek looked to the skies, they beheld in the cosmos their being; past, present and future and, in much the same manner as the mariners of old who drew their bearings from the skies in their navigation, so did the Anishinaubaek derive their directions from the skies for the moral course of their lives.

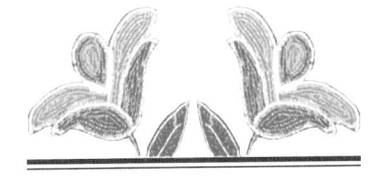

"I'M GLAD GOD IS NOT PERFECT"

Basil H. Johnston, O.Ont., LLD., B.A. © Sept. 15, 1983

"I'm Glad God Is Not Perfect"

Some years ago a fellow teacher who had gone camping to Cape Croker, my home, remarked to me on his return in the staff-room "Basil! I just got back from your reserve where my family and I camped over the week-end. Beautiful place! Beautiful! Those big bluffs behind; the trees in the camp ground … so tall; maple, beech, oak! and that Georgian Bay water … so clear, pure! Hardly any place nicer than Cape Croker in Bruce Peninsula. But Basil, the only thing that bothered me were the front yards; they're awful, full of weeds. Why don't your people cut those weeds; your homes and your reserve would be so much nicer. What's wrong with your people anyway?"

At the time I didn't pay too much attention to my colleague's remarks for, knowing his general good nature, I took it for granted that he meant well, and besides, my people had never been too much offended by thistles, dandelions, burdock, plantain, mullein, sweet-grass, wild roses, milkweed, buttercups and assorted grasses and hay that grew in abundant profusion in everyone's yard over the entire reserve. What was unsightly and offensive to my colleague and others like him was to us not at all disagreeable.

Since my fellow-teacher's complaint on that day many years ago, I can now report that almost all of the people at Cape Croker have now acquired lawn-mowers and almost as assiduously as urban dwellers, weekly cut their weeds, transforming what had once been little fields into neat and tidy lawns.

That my colleague would be nettled by the indiscriminate and desultory growth of plants that he and many others regarded as weeds was understandable; he was a mathematician and as such was completely committed to the extirpation of disorder and confusion, in order to obtain precision and regularity. Besides, he was a city-type, accustomed to life and work in rectangular buildings and square rooms designed according to precise mathematical measurements, and familiar only with uniform lawns, hedges and flower-beds, geometrical in layout. Any state or condition other than uniform in pattern unsettled my friend.

My colleagues in the History and English departments in the same school were just as obsessed with order and precision, as were those teaching in the

Science departments, though their notions of precision, which they called perfection, and the means of attaining it were different.

It was not until one of my students turned in an examination paper that was without error and earned a mark of 100 percent, which I duly wrote across the face of the examination paper and entered it in the report card, that I realized just how strongly my colleagues felt about perfection and how forcefully they resisted perfection of any kind. "How can you give 100 percent? No one's perfect" I was reprimanded.

Thereafter I heard similar sentiments expressed during promotion meetings and during discussions in the staff lounge. "She's got everything right, but you can't give her 100 percent … nobody's perfect;" "There has to be something wrong someplace;" "He doesn't deserve a 100 percent;" "I never give a perfect mark!" Now whether it was ordinary pettiness or genuine regard to uphold perfection in its pristine state that prompted most teachers to refuse to accord to anyone 100 percent is hard to say. In any event, owing to the mistaken notion that 100 percent was no different from perfection but was one and the same with it, more time and talent was spent in looking for flaws and errors than in discovering or promoting merit.

There was not a chance that students could attain 100 percent so long as 100 percent was equated with perfection, even were they to score all full, half, quarter, eighth and sixteenth marks as prescribed in a marking scheme that was intended to secure uniform marking by teachers, as well as to prevent perfect marks.

Critics and reviewers are more preoccupied with perfectionism than are teachers. When I first aspired to write I sought the advice of Cyril Davies, editor of the Board of Trade Journal and friend, as to the best manner of learning the craft. Besides recommending "The King's English" by Fowler, Mr. Davies suggested that I read reviews and critiques. Following Cy's advice, I read and studied reviews and critiques devotedly for about two years in the hope of learning what were the merits of the writings of a Hemingway, a Steinbeck, a Wouk, a Uris, so that I might acquire some principles of the craft of good writing. It was a waste of time. I learned only how badly these authors wrote.

At the outset I did not understand why writers of reviews and critiques were more willing to damn and condemn than to commend or acclaim. I now believe that I know the reason. Ever since Adam and Eve deprived their descendants of their legacy to the Garden of Eden and bequeathed to them a flawed world by their commission of the original sin, men and women have found fault and endeavoured, by stamping it out, to restore mankind to its previous innocent state. To cast stones at a woman for her sins, instead of withholding the first pitch in accordance with Christ's counsel "Let him who is without sin cast the first stone," is firmly rooted in West European heritage as a vicarious act of vengeance directed against Adam and Eve.

And reviewers and critics are as fervent as are members of the Holy Orders in their search for and condemnation of flaw and imperfection.

There is, of course, another reason for the fixation on faults, flaws, defects as means of judging the works or character of another. Imperfections, or whatever term may be used to describe them, are easier to perceive than are merits, and it obviates giving credit for the good work of another.

Not only is it fairly easy to declare that no one is perfect or that no book is without flaw, it is also safe to make such statements. By making such a generalization that cannot be confuted, the critic or reviewer is protecting his rump from a scorching.

And though it may well serve the critic's need to judge every work or performance in terms of perfection, the critique or review can seldom be a dependable or valid measure of worth. Were authors, artists and performers to aspire for perfection in their works and performances, then the evaluation of their works and performances on the basis of perfection would be a valid one. However, it is unlikely that any writer or artist would be so presumptuous as to yearn to write the perfect poem or paint the perfect picture or put on the perfect performance. Were an author or artist to achieve perfection, there would be nothing more to write or to present, would there? I prefer to believe that poets and pianists, composers and dancers, playwrights and actresses had purpose other than the attainment of perfection and that is of creating or re-creating through writing, carving, painting, singing something beautiful, accurate, cheerful, romantic, apt, dismal, fanciful or realistic in order to inform or to please, to comfort or encourage, to amuse or to move the minds and spirits of men and women. It is on the basis of how well they accomplished what they set out to do that their works and performances ought to be adjudged. Without some reference to the merits of a work or performance, a critique or a review remains a prejudiced opinion.

There is perhaps no institution more concerned with perfection than is a church or religious order for the simple reason that it is their mandate to bring about the moral growth and spiritual betterment of mankind. When a clergyman or woman talks of perfection, he or she speaks of moral perfection that exists only in Heaven and is an attribute of God.

Now while clergymen and women tell us that only God is perfect, and that Heaven is a state of perfection, they offer hope that all may some day attain Heaven if all were to abide by the commandments and to excise all their sins through confession and penance. To die in the state of grace still does not gain automatic admission into Heaven; so deeply embedded in the soul of human beings is sin inherited from the act of disobedience of Adam and Eve that all must pass through Purgatory for purification by fire. "Only God is perfect; men and women and all their works are imperfect."

Since that time the belief that perfection in all forms is to be found only in Heaven, and that neither man nor woman is capable of attaining or expressing perfection has dominated all and every understanding of the meaning of the term. But there is perfection, not in the moral or theological order perhaps, but perfection nevertheless in things mensurable or aesthetic that men and women perceive from time to time by revelation. Carpenters will declare the frame of a building to be "perfect," as will a hostess of the setting of a table. Lovers will describe an evening with a setting sun or a full moon saying, "it's a perfect night," just as chaperones will readily say "they were perfect" of their charges. Be it doctor or mechanic or watch-maker, all will pronounce "perfect" upon the health of a thing or in the operation of a piece of machinery. Though perfection may have a higher meaning, and exist only in Heaven or in the after-life, things of this world ought not to be measured against it.

In thinking about perfection in its various aspects, it is a good thing that it is God rather than man or woman who presides over and determines what perfection ought to be; men and women are too intolerant when it comes to perfection or imperfection.

Had Adam and Eve not sinned, humankind would not have been burdened with all the troubles of attaining it. But they did sin, and humankind has ever had to endure; to bear imperfection.

Fortunately for all, there are men and women generous enough in spirit, as was Brother van der Moor S.J. who, on the occasion of my first ploughing at age 13, said, after he had scanned the furrows, "Not bad for the first time" without once adverting to perfection, human or divine.

Suppose ... suppose that the world and all the creatures upon it were to be re-created; and suppose that God had engaged as consultants in this great project engineers, architects and designers, all mathematicians. What would have been the result? What kind of world?

We have but to draw attention to humankind's inventions, manufactures and designs to imagine what kind of world and beings upon it that engineers and architects would re-create to correspond to their notions of perfection.

Just imagine. All the stars and heavenly bodies would be transfixed in perfect rows in the sky; all seasons would be precisely quartered, all days and nights of equal duration. Plants, according to species, would sit by line in groves; trees would grow and decline at the same rate, bud and blossom at the same time, bear the identical number and form of leaves and fruit, and be perfectly symmetrical, much like artificial Christmas trees. Animals such as the bear or the tiger would resemble plush toys, teddy bears and toy tigers with gentle dispositions. As for human beings, well ... they would either be cast out of plastic or some metal to exist and operate like the robot R2D2 in Star Wars, perfect metal clones. Everything and everyone would be perfectly created in the same sense in which ball bearings are perfectly moulded in order to fulfill their functions perfectly. Perfect? Yes. Beautiful? Hardly.

Next suppose that God had had the counsel of scholars, assuming that such men and women could suspend quibbling among themselves or with God as to what constituted perfection just long enough to get the project underway. What kind of world? What kind of human being? What kind of conditions? We can do not much better than to refer to Ovid's conception of the perfect or ideal world to furnish us with an idea of what scholars or poets would propose in place of the old. The Golden Age.

The Age was formed of gold; in those first days
No law or force was needed; men did right.
Freely; without duress they kept their word
No punishment or fear of it; no threats
Inscribed on brazen tablets; no crowds crawled
Beseeching mercy from a lofty judge
For without law or judge all men were safe.
High on its native hills the pine tree stood,
Unlopped as yet, nor yet compelled to cross
Ocean's wide waves and help none leave their homes.
Towns had no moats; no horns of winding brass
Nor trumpets straight, no swords nor shields existed.
The nations dozed through ages of soft time,
Safe without armies; while the earth herself
Untouched by spade or ploughshare, freely gave,
As of her own volition, all men needed;
And men were well content with what she gave
Unforced and uncompelled; they found the fruit
Of the arbutus bush and cornel-cherries,
Gathered wild berries from the mountain sides,
Eating ripe fruit plucked from the thorny canes,
And acorns as they fell from Jove's wide oak,
Spring lasted all year long; the warm west wind
Played gently over flowers sprung from no seed:
Soon too the untilled earth brought forth profuse
Her crops of grain; and fields uncultivated
Whitened beneath their stalks of bearded wheat
Streams flowed profuse, now milk, now nectar, and
The living oak poured streams of golden honey.

And to make sure that men and women were "well content" not only in the economic and social orders, but also in the intellectual sphere, there would be established an Academy of Absolutes or an Academy of Perfection somewhat akin to the Academie Français but much stricter, that would impose standards near to perfection on all sculptors, painters, poets, playwrights, dancers, musicians and writers.

Perfect? Ideal? Yes. Fulfilling? Not likely.

Lastly, what if theologians, men or women, had counselled God in the reorganization of the world and humankind? Their sole concern would be with the moral order rather than the material, and the re-creation of a state approximating that which existed in the Garden of Eden.

What existed then was a Utopia in which humankind's materials needs were so amply satisfied in all respects that men and women lived in perpetual peace and harmony. Such a state would have to be restored in order to reduce, insofar as possible, any and all occasions for temptation to sin.

Even in this Utopian state the behaviour of men and women would be strictly regulated by Codes and Rituals, customs and habits, form and tradition, administered by a College of Moral Modification and even by a Conservatory of Behaviour Modification. By law strictly enforced all men and women would read and master the codes, attend church, synagogue or temple every day; confess frequently, and maybe wear sack-cloth or ashes as a sign of their sinfulness and penitence until all or nearly all thoughts of malice or acts of selfishness had been removed from one's being. All men and women would be disciplined and trained to obey commands and laws, in much the same way soldiers are moulded to comply instantaneously. Thus it would be by means of observing laws and codes and by the slow excision of sin in stages that moral perfection, insofar as it can be attained on this earth, would be achieved.

Purgatory would be retained, of course, as the final stage in the process of expunging the last remaining vestige of sin in the soul of man or woman to render the initiate fit for Paradise.

Perfect? Yes, ... but is perfection acquired by excision of imperfection, or virtue by the removal of sin, or pure soul state by abstraction in Purgatory?

As perfect or as near perfection as are some of man's creations such as ball-bearings and robots, or even artificial Christmas trees, and as well intended as are the means for bringing this state about, there is something missing in the creations themselves. Though the ball-bearing may be perfect in form, it is devoid of beauty; though a Utopian state may be ideal, it would seem to stultify growth; and though human conduct may be without blemish by way of removal of sin, it is not necessarily virtuous.

There is here a paradox: on the one hand humankind may create objects of perfection such as for example the ball-bearing, but failed to impress beauty upon it; and on the other, may have failed to attain perfection in their paintings or poetry yet succeeded in occasioning beauty, a paradox that suggests that the term "perfection" may be and ought to be understood in a sense other than that which is obtained by excision, removal of fault, or abstraction, that which is without flaw.

We have but to look at the world about us to realize that God must have had something other than perfection in mind when he created this world and the beings upon it. Take the tree, for instance. He made it of a substance fragile and pliant; in shape bent and warped of trunk and limb; and He crowned the trees with twigged and fretted blossoms with frayed and curled leaves. And He planted these to grow not in columns in groves but in woods and forests. And yet, from warps and bumps and frets and drabs He conferred a beauty. So with everything else upon this earth and above. God worked from flaws and imperfections, at least in the human understanding, to create beauty and to give sense to things, and that is what I think He had in mind.

What God, or Kitchi-Manitou created was not perfection by excision, but beauty through growth and harmony. It is humankind who has fostered the notion that perfection is embodied in flawlessness which is to be attained by abstraction, and has imposed this notion upon God and his fellow human beings. Rather, it is from the principal characteristics of creation; growth, self-healing and beauty, that mankind might understand and pursue perfection.

And that is why I write, not with any disrespect, but with reverence: "I am glad that God is not Perfect."

What's Your Dialect?

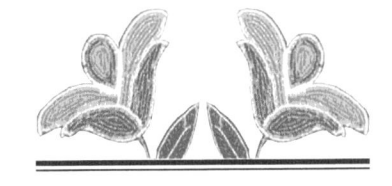

Basil H. Johnston, O.Ont., LLD., B.A. © Oct. 18, 1983

What's Your Dialect?

Whatever answer we give to the question "What's your nationality?" will lead to yet another question that will differ each time depending on the interests and the background of the questioner.

Often "I'm an Indian, Ojibway (Chippewa)" or more correctly "Anishinaubae" will evoke surprise expressed by "I thought you were Korean," or some other sentiment such as "How very interesting; I've always been interested in the Native peoples." Now, to be mistaken for a Korean or Chinese or Japanese or Philipino is perfectly natural as they are, I'm given to understand, related though somewhat distantly to us. But … the tone with which "I thought you were …" is sometimes expressed suggesting disappointment and the conversation peters out for lack of further interest.

On occasion "I'm an Indian, an Ojibway" will provoke "What the hell do you people want anyway? Why should you be entitled to rights over and above what the rest of us enjoy?" and an argument ensues between two antagonists who are usually equally misinformed about the subject of rights or the issues. The question is then political.

There are times when the question "What's your nationality?" is motivated by admirers of ornaments only as a sly means of satisfying their curiosity about the necklace or ring that you and I may have been wearing at that moment, and there are two ways of answering the follow-up question "What does it mean?" One is to deliver a long explanation, either true or false, about the origin and the symbolism of the ornament; the other is to say that the object was made from the shin-bone of a White man whom your father had slain during a massacre in the previous century. The kind of answer given depends upon mood.

If, however, an academic, particularly one with linguistics training or a smattering thereof, were to ask, "What's your nationality or tribal affiliation?" he or she must next inquire, "What dialect?" But that's to be expected, isn't it, from people who do not speak the language and who may want to show that they do know something about some of the differences that exist in the Native languages, and it is astonishing just how authoritatively these academics can pronounce upon and influence the course of the Native languages, especially when few, if any, speak any one of the languages.

Now this is the subject that I wish to address this morning. In preparation for this paper I have searched the language and asked the elders what term, if any, was used to denote "dialect"; and so far as search carried me and so far as the Elders knew, there was no word comparable to "dialect" in the Anishinaubae language. What they used to say, according to my informants, was "pekaun igoh pungee," or "just a little different" in describing those differences in accent and in usage that occur in speech. And as far as we know these differences in dialect did not matter enough to our ancestors to prejudice their talking to one another.

It is only in recent years, within the past 30 years, that dialect, which is really a small matter in itself, has become big, and I rather suspect that it has something to do with the decrease in the number of people speaking their mother tongues. Many of our own Native brothers and sisters who have not had the good fortune of having been taught their language can now only say "that is not my dialect" in a kind of apologetic way to hide the fact that they either do not speak it at all, or very little. And as the number of speakers of the Native languages grows less and less, the matter of preserving and extending language grows greater and greater, each group naturally wants its dialect to be preserved. Dialects have become bigger than the languages themselves, as if the parts are more important than the whole.

So big has dialect or language become that it has been removed from the home into schools and universities where it has become a subject… and big business. Linguists armed with tape recorders and questionnaires have gone in the field from reserve to reserve for brief periods to collect word lists and record stories, and then to return to headquarters in some Department of Education or to university to write their theses and teach courses. Universities have established chairs and departments not so much for the teaching of language itself as German or French are taught, but for the study of linguistics and research into orthographies. Besides these basic functions, universities sponsor and even conduct seminars, conferences and three and six week crash courses in methodology. For universities, "dialects" are the fat by which linguistic departments have grown big and strong.

Now instead of, or in addition to, offering courses of limited scope in linguistics, or conducting research of little value in dialect, universities could render a greater service to students, Native and non-Native, and to the Native languages and the community by providing courses in Native literature and eloquence. That would be something, wouldn't it, for universities to appreciate literature and eloquence above dialect just as our ancestors did?

And because our forebears admired and valued eloquence and imagination in narration and oratory, they probably paid no more attention to dialect or peculiar accents than we do today when we hear an Italian or a Chinese or a Catherine Deneuve speak English. It's to give understanding and to understand that's important, isn't it?

What difference does it make if one says, "Where do you come from?" another, "Where are you from?" still another, "Where do you hail from?" and yet another, "Where do you make your home?" They all mean the same thing, don't they? You understand what the question means, don't you? You don't take issue with any of the expressions, do you? And suppose one Anishinaubae were to ask "Aundih abi-ondjibauyin?" and another "Aundih abi-ondjeeyin?" and another "Ahneesh omauh ae-daneeyin?" or "Ahneesh omauh ae-indauyin?" and yet another "Aundih abi-ondaukooweeyin?" or "Ahneesh omauh aubeetumun?" And suppose that the questioner uttered the question in different tones or even with a different accent; would it make any difference? They all mean the same thing, do they not? Even though the expressions may be unfamiliar, the words are well known because they are part of the language and a part of us. And who is to say that one is more important than another, or that one ought to be excluded from our daily speech. If you understand them, isn't it all that is necessary?

How then are we to account for the differences in expression, in accent, in syntax, in diction, if indeed we are to account for them. Really it is no great mystery; the cause is to be found in the very richness of the language itself and in the fertility of the Anishinaubae mind. The language is immense; it is only the vocabulary of the individual that is limited.

What made us brothers and sisters; what made us Anishinaubae and what bound our people as one was not religion nor an ideology nor an allegiance to a flag or a single leader; none of these, but rather it was language and common understandings of life that were framed and expressed by previous generations in myth, legend, chant and word which have been bestowed upon us as our legacy. As I listen to a storyteller tell a story I sometimes fancy that his voice and his words are but echoes of a storyteller long dead but whose words and stories have survived to cheer, inspire and guide us. It is by virtue of speaking the same language and espousing common beliefs that we are one people, descendants of like ancestors.

With ever fewer people speaking their Native tongue, and as the only contribution of the present generation to the rich legacy of tribal literature seems only to have been "to record before they die out," ought we not try with every ounce of energy and with every shade of talent to enrich our literature and to restore our language as a bond between us as it was intended to be instead of demeaning it and breaking it down into dialects?

It is a sad thing to go to an Indian centre in a strange city to seek companionship with one who speaks the language and to find none; and what a happy occasion when one or several are to be found. It is a sad thing to go into a community of 1600 to learn that only 100 or so of the elderly still remember the language. It is a sad thing to go into a village where no one remembers a word. It is a sad but natural thing to hear an Anishinaubae say "them" in referring to his fellow tribesmen, natural because the bond of language has been broken and new modes of thoughts acquired in another language; sadder still to contemplate is that strong as language may be, it is always one generation from extinction.

Yet as another old man or old woman dies leaving one less speaker to utter and uphold the language, there are those who take exception to accent. "Oh that's Odauwauh!" "That's Pottawatomi," "That's not our dialect." "It's going to take me a month to undo the dialect that you've taught them." Instead of teaching the next newborn to speak the language in order to give continuity to the tribe and benefit to the child, people quibble about dialect.

It's rather late, and sad to say too late in some instances, for the survival of the language of the tribe for people to be squabbling about dialect. Were the language as sound today as it was 40 and 50 years ago, there might be some benefit in the study of dialect. But languages are fading and in these circumstances the first task, insofar as we are capable and insofar as our people are willing, is to restore the language to its former healthy state, and in order to do this we ought to borrow from one another and to assist one another until the job is done. In the meantime it would not hurt to consign dialect to the farthest end of the least used filing cabinet in the linguistics department of the nearest university or museum.

For what is at issue today? It is no less than the survival of tribal language and the whole body of tribal knowledge that is embodied in the oral literature. That is what is at issue today, not dialect. And what is at stake? It is your identity, my brothers and sisters, nothing less. What you stand to lose is that which makes you Anishinaubae, Dakota, Cree, Assiniboine, different, unique and distinct, in language, outlook and in appearance.

Now if our language and our identity are in jeopardy, ought not the people who have a direct stake in those two aspects of our future have a greater part in determining the direction that Native language teaching takes by providing advice in the formulation of policy and curriculum? But we have today a situation which to my knowledge has no parallel anywhere else; linguists and others who have no stake except a peripheral kind in a Native language and, to the best of my knowledge, none of whom speaks the language, serve as principal consultants to Departments of Education and to Boards of Education in matters of Native language education. And what is the result? A linguistic approach with emphasis upon morphemics, dialects, and the gender of words. At this stage in the state of many Native languages what is required is the teaching of the spoken word.

The basic principle in teaching a language is to teach it the way our grandparents and parents taught us our language and the way other parents and grandparents taught their children their languages. They talked to us; we listened; they spoke to one another and we listened until we began to understand the meaning of words and to unlock the meaning of sentences. They opened our ears to the magic of sound and the mystery of words. There was nothing fancy or clever or profound in their teachings but we imitated them, poorly perhaps at first, until at last we could speak without ever having known what was animative or frigative or dubitative. I know of no better way of teaching or learning a language than to follow that principle in a classroom, even though the classroom is a setting different from that of a home.

There was something else our grandparents and parents did at the same time as they taught us the sound of words; they wove them together into ideas and images, they wove them into stories which gave us the essential concepts about life and about ourselves. Words were not animate or inanimate, but they represented ideas and together, understandings. And when our parents were done, it was up to us to enlarge that legacy.

The trouble, you see, with a linguistics approach is that the word is taught not in its essential meaning nor in its place in stories to impart concepts, but as sound or even a plaything only, and the quicker that we abandon this course, the better it will be for students.

Let us suspend for a while conducting field surveys to establish that because this reserve uses for the term mother "n'gushih," and that reserve uses "n'd'ogeem"; another uses "n'gah" and yet another uses "n'dodoom," and still a different community prefers "n'mamauh" that there are indeed different and separate dialects, in order to regain that love and respect that comes only from an understanding of the essential meaning of words that everyone used to possess but which none but the very old now possess. Let us examine the words that make up our language to discover what it is that gives them vitality and substance. Then we may come to appreciate what we are losing, and then maybe we may redirect our thinking and our efforts to tasks that are important in the preservation of our languages.

We need no more than a few examples to illustrate that behind and beneath the general meanings of words that we take for granted and seldom think about are concepts that only the very old could understand and explain, and this is so for the simple reason that as only the very old can see stars and constellations that the young cannot, so can they understand meanings within the meanings of words and stories that are hidden to the young. Take, for instance, the word "manitou" which has been taken to mean spirit. Were the word "manitou" to have denoted "spirit" it could not have been predicated of rock, plant or other being. But it has another meaning wider and even more basic than "spirit" that enables it to be used in reference to rock, plant and even man or woman, and that meaning is "mystery." It refers to those things such as properties, essences, matter, substances, powers, duties which cannot be understood or explained. Unable to explain what properties a plant possessed to confer healing, the Anishinaubaek said of it "manitouwun." Even the translation of "Kitchi-manitou" into English "the Great Mystery" has a dimension and element that "Great

Spirit" has not. Consider the word "aki" or "aski" in Cree, meaning land, earth, soil, ground, continent, as it forms the core, the muscle, the fibre of other words. A part of "akiwaehnzee" meaning old man derives from "aki." "Aki" or earth combined with "waehnzee" meaning leaning or upon, bending toward, relying on, produces the concept of and old man bending ever closer to the earth which describes one of the results of aging. By uniting "n'weedji" (with, in company with, together) with "aki" (earth, soil, land, etc.), and with "waehn" the word "n'weedji-akiwaehn" or friend is formed. Essentially the word for friend means he or she with whom I share the land (earth) or he or she who shares the land (earth) with me. The word for medicine is "mashki-aki"; "mashki" meaning strength, power, might conjoined with aki-earth yields "strength of the earth," describing the process by which the earth transmits its healing power through a plant to the sick. "Aki" plus "eewae," a verbalizer if one may call it that, meaning "to make or render" begets "akeewae" or he or she goes home. What a marvellous concept behind the word "akeewae," to return to one's earth or land. The word for young man, "oshkinawae" derives from "oshki" meaning new or fresh and from "nawae" meaning cheek, gives new or fresh cheek, an apt description for a youth. For young women, "oshkineegiquae" is made up of "oshki" (new, fresh), "neegih" (growth, budding, maturing) and "quae" (woman, female), or a new growing woman. And there are a number of words like "w'abi-izhau" whose meaning "he or she comes" is evident but whose component parts "abi" (here, in this place) and "izhauh" (he, she goes) produces, if translated literally, an awkward expression somewhat similar to "there he (she) goes coming this way." From these few examples, and there are many more, may be gained some insight as to the nature and character of the Anishinaubae language in the construction of words and the concepts they embody.

As interesting as etymology may be, we did not and we do not learn language that way. We got to know the words and their meanings from their use in some context, usually in a story. At the same time we got to learn the broader concepts of life from those same stories.

I do not think that we can improve much the methods of teaching language or about life that our ancestors used, even though we have the advantage of books and paper and machines. And if their methods served them well, ought we not emulate them?

They told stories, and the children learned easily and quickly and readily the words and their meanings, the stories and their meanings until the words became a part of them through speech. They learned easily because they trusted their parents and their grandparents, and they learned quickly because they accepted the truth of the word and the story, and they learned readily because they loved Nanabush and Weessaukeechauk and feared Weendigo. They learned best because they were encouraged, and they learned naturally, step-by-step, year-by-year. It's said that children learn more quickly than do adults, and I suppose that if this is so, it is because their minds are not cluttered up with fears of animates, frigatives, glottal stops, moods, subjunctives, syntax or even pronunciation, but are free to receive new knowledge. They know that it takes time. And when they listen to a story, they give themselves completely to it, caring nothing about structure or character development or plot or nuances; they laugh, they cry, they are glad, they are sad, they rejoice and they are alarmed, and they have a strong sense of truth and beauty and fair play. Can we not teach language and story in the same way?

Word and story are inseparable, and even though a word may have its own gender, habitat, mood, voice, sound, and may even exist by itself with its own meaning and concept, it is merely a word and not much more. But in conjunction with other words it takes on even more force and bears fuller meaning, while at the same time it enriches other words. Words give force to stories as stories give vitality to words. And that is why stories impart the meanings of words and ideas and concepts better than do dictionaries. The whole of the stories of a people constitutes its literature, written or otherwise.

As long as the language was strong our literature was vigorous, ever growing, always unwritten but ever remembered because it was engraved in the minds of the elders and planted in the minds of the young. Much of it has now been written and recorded on tape, in English, deprived of its essential meanings. For quite a while now our literature has not really grown as it did in former times, owing in large part to the increasing disuse of our Native language.

Now if it is inseparable from the word, the story must be the basis for teaching the language. But few are available in print in our Native languages; such being the case the duty falls upon those of us fortunate enough to have retained our language to provide that material by retranslating the stories into our own Native languages and, if we have no talent, to compose new ones. I do not think that there is a better way of keeping our language and literature alive and strong than by writing it, putting it on tape for the benefit of students and teachers.

And for those who have for some reason or other never been given an opportunity of learning their language, could they not spend one hour a day in acquiring it?

What of Ministries or Departments of Education, universities or colleges, and museums and similar institutions? How can they serve? Many have already instituted programs for the Native languages, but they either have not gone far enough or they have not gone in the right direction. Briefly I would like to see Ministries or Departments of Education allow more classroom time for Native language instruction, as well as providing the means for the publication of Native language books; universities should require that its linguists be proficient in one of the languages and offer courses in language which would be mandatory for Native teaching and methodology, and museums should collect stories on tape and paper as readily as they do snowshoes, bows and arrows and other artifacts and make them available. As Native languages and Native literature constitute part of the heritage of this country, this nation's institutions must do what they can to preserve and ensure their growth.

Let us for the time being suspend this study of differences in dialect or in linguistics and rather say, as the old Native people used to say, "Keeshpin geewaussitooyaek, aubawaewaenimishik; kauween ondjitah, mee gauh izhi-kikinoomaukooyaun." "If you do not quite understand me, forgive me; it is not deliberate for that is the way I was taught."

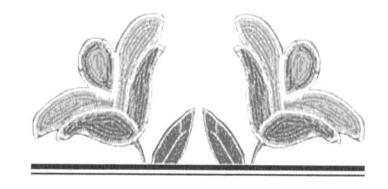

How Do We Learn Language?

What Do We Learn?

Basil H. Johnston, O.Ont., LLD., B.A. © November 18, 1985

How Do We Learn Language?

What Do We Learn?

There are, of course, many ways a case may be argued or a thesis presented. The matter of establishing the bond between language and literature for the purpose of improving language instruction is no different. For in logic, both language and literature may well be considered as separate and independent, as if they were unrelated. But to treat these topics as if they had no bearing one upon the other is not representative of the kinship between them, nor the manner of their growth and development. It is precisely because language has been separated from literature in Native language programs for teachers and students that language studies have by and large failed.

Were language to be considered not as an element unrelated to literature, but as an integral constituent of it, the philosophic basis of language instruction would undergo change. And were such practical matters as the manner and progression of learning, and what other knowledge besides speech is acquired in the course of learning a language taken into account, current methods and systems would be set aside, and others more in keeping with the natural mode and order of learning language be instituted.

The questions to be asked are, how do we learn language, and what do we learn from language? Think of how it was when you were a child; think of how it is with children. Think of how you learned your language, and think of what you learned. Think of how children learn speech.

They do not have trained teachers; they do not have formal lessons; they do not learn in classrooms; they do not refer to texts; they do not labour over homework. They know nothing of grammar or linguistics, or of phonics or sound systems. They have none of the advantages that modern language students have, or studying in private carrels and wearing headphones and following a program. Yet they learn.

How can this be? How can a child or anyone learn without some preparation, without a scheme? I think that children learn easily and readily because they listen and give wholeheartedly of themselves to sound.

Even while they are yet fetal beings, without any means of knowing the world outside the womb it is said, and so I believe, that children can hear. If that is so, then hearing may well be regarded as prior to and even more essential than are the other senses in learning. And hearing remains the principal means by which children get to know the world and the other beings in it during the first few months of their lives. For infants, there is little else but sound and touch; they can only listen.

And what is it that the infant hears? What does an infant listen to? Initially, I think that a babe hears nothing but a cacophony of sounds, unable to distinguish the rustle of leaves from the crackle of fire. At first, to a baby, the peal of thunder, the pound of breakers upon a shore, and the drum of partridge wings will be the same, differing only in volume. They will hear the sounds of varying pitch and harmony, tone and intensity. But it is mainly the human voice that an infant will listen to. The mother talks, the child listens. The parents talk, the child listens. Parents and their friends talk, the child listens. Other children talk, the child listens. Other than to cry and eat on occasion, the child does little else but listen.

Then, by degrees, the child begins to distinguish between one sound and another, and begins to understand that sounds have meanings, and that sounds with meanings are words. The child may indeed learn that "this is a foot" and that "this is a hand," and that a distant bark is that made by a "dog," but for the most part the mother and the parents go about their business of talking about the day's events, or telling stories in the evenings without explaining the meanings of words or discussing stories. To do so would be pointless to the child, but the child listens.

Then one day, two and a half years after its birth, and upwards to 6,000 hours of listening, the child utters his first word in imitation of his mother or father. What word the child utters is not important, nor is how the word pronounced any more than cute. What is important and cause for joy for the parents is that the child has spoken. And the point at which a child attempts speech for the first time occurs when the child's hearing has become acute enough to allow the child to discern the difference between sounds, and when the child begins to understand that sounds have meanings; not before. From the first word the child proceeds quickly to others, loosening his tongue in the process.

Still the child listens. In the days and months that follow the child adds to his vocabulary and to his understanding quickly and surely. No longer is his hearing and speech simple, but complex; the child's mind begins to grasp and form ideas.

That is how you and I learned our language; that is how other children learn their languages.

And even though we knew something of words and ideas, still we listened. That is how it was in our youth; that is how it is with other children. When children's vocabulary is large enough, they begin to listen to stories, and they begin to learn something of their heritage and culture.

Now, as children and youth were learning their tribe's traditions and customs and understandings, they were also learning more about their own language.

What the children and youth of one generation learned of the past and of the knowledge of the tribe came through story. By custom and tradition our tribal storytellers told certain stories only in winter. These winter night gatherings were more than storytelling socials; they were meetings in which tradition, heritage, custom and culture were passed on to the youth.

The old storytellers, old men and old women, must have been endowed with insight and originality to create stories that were both whimsical and full of meaning at the same time. They created comic characters, Nana'b'oozoo and Pukawiss, and they invested comic situations for human beings, as well for the deities; and they envisioned manitous and monsters, and they described heroes and cowards. All of the storytellers had a way with words, minting new terms in the course of their narration by combining prefixes and suffixes in new and unusual ways.

Listeners loved to laugh as much as they loved to reflect. First laughter, then thought. But it is precisely because our tribal stories are comical and evoke laughter that they have never been taken seriously outside the tribe. They have been regarded as juvenile, fit only for juvenile minds.

But behind and beneath the comic characters and the comic situations and the comic descriptions existed the real meaning of the story.

When the storyteller told of the great flood and the re-creation of the world from a pawfull of soil obtained by the muskrat from the bottom of the flood waters, the storyteller was illuminating in the most dramatic way possible how men and women may create their beings and their spheres from the pawfull of talent or potentiality lying within the depths of their soul-spirits. The storyteller was telling the story not so much for the amusement of children as he was describing what the tribe understood of human growth and development. Or the storyteller may recount the story of Nana'b'oozoo's hunting expedition with the wolves in order to learn to hunt first hand under the tutelage of one of the foremost hunters in the forest. To hear how Nana'b'oozoo trips over his own tail, or how he too soon tires in the pursuit of his quarry, a moose, and must rest, and how he will not follow the advice and the example of his tutor because his tutor is only a wolf may be regarded as juvenile, but the story exemplifies an aspect of human nature that seems to apply to humankind in general. In recounting the story the narrator does not explain that Nana'b'oozoo was like every other human being in following his own inclination rather than the advice or the example of another being. And Nana'b'oozoo was no different from any other human being who is deluded by long bushy tails and speed and grace. It may take years and many stories, but the child will begin to see in Nana'b'oozoo human nature; the child will see himself and he will begin to understand why Nana'b'oozoo suffers misadventures.

No one tells the child what the stories mean. The storyteller does not explain that Nana'b'oozoo is every man, every woman. The Elders do not comment on human conduct. To the storyteller and the tribe, the story tells itself. It is for the child and each individual to seek that morsel of understanding, and to draw his own inferences and start fashioning his being and his world. And in letting the listener interpret his stories in his own way and according to the scope of his intellect, the storyteller and the Elders of the tribe trusted in the common sense of the child to draw interpretations that were both reasonable and sensible.

In the coming years the child would elicit more and more meanings from stories, and ever more quickly see the point in the story.

When that child sat before the storyteller to listen to stories, that child gave his spirit and his mind and himself to the story and the storyteller. Next to the children sat adults who listened to the same story, who listened in their own way, as one day the child would listen, but for the present the child was hearing something new and fresh. As they listened to stories and learned about battles and migrations, about the origin of day and night, or the meaning of the call of owls, children were also learning more language. They may not have known it but they were learning about the vitality of words as words took on different shades of meanings in different contexts or lost some meaning in still another context. The children may not have known it, but words take on new dimensions only in conjunction and by union with other words. A word may indeed have its own meaning, gender, habitat, mood, voice, sound, and exist alone, but it is only in relation with other words that it can acquire greater sense and impart sense to other words. This, then, is what children and youth and all of us learn about language in the course of a story.

Words have range, but they also have limits to their meaning; they can express only so much, and I suppose that this is so because men and women have limits to what they can know and how they can describe it. The word "w'daeb-awae" describes the tribe's fundamental notion as to the limits of perception and description. W'daeb-awae, in its literal sense conveys the notion "he/she casts his/her voice to the very limits of its range." It refers to what one can know and what one can say. When a man or a woman is said to be speaking to the ends of knowledge and to the ends of language, they are said to be speaking the truth. According to this term, and according to the tribe, the best that a speaker can do, and the most that the listener can expect, is not absolute truth but the highest degree of accuracy. Besides, one's senses may be easily beguiled and even deceived by bushy tails. It is better to say that "it appears to be" or "it is said" or that "the probability is high that" as the old people used to do with "eedoog."

On learning that an acquaintance whom I had not seen for some years was in Toronto, I asked my friend what our acquaintance was doing. "W'anookeedoog" my friend replied, meaning that our acquaintance was in all probability working. By nature the man was a good worker, and it would be hard for him to survive in Toronto without some occupation. However, there was a possibility that our acquaintance was not working. One could no more be sure about remote matters than one could say for certain that a person staggering down the road was inebriated. To the old people truth, insofar as a person could know and express it, was sacred. A person who spoke what was within his knowledge was trusted and respected; one who spoke about things he or she knew nothing of was said to be speaking in circles, "w'geewinimoh."

A word is elastic. It changes form, it changes moods, it changes tenses. It even changes its own structure by adding to itself and sometimes by subtracting from itself. That is the magic and mystery of words, and yet children will understand that word whatever be its size, shape or colour from its place in a sentence and in the story. Eventually he will get to know "w'inaendum" which means he or she thinks, whether it is commingled with or is garbled by other sounds. From w'min-inaendum, w'kitchi-inaendum, w'geezhi-aendum, w'mauni-aendum, w'kishki-aendum, w'maunaud-aendum, w'banaud-aendum, w'geemood-aendum, w'geebaud-aendum, w'moozhig-aendum, w'nishinaud-aendum, w'naunaugataw-aendum, w'zaum-aendum, w'nigaud-aendum, w'chaunim-aendum and other forms of "inaendum" the child will know the meaning of the word, even though he has not heard it before. In the same way the child will learn, as you and I learned, that "w'abi-izhauh" means he/she comes here, although "abi-" means in this place and "w'izhauh" means he/she goes; as he will say "w'mino-nawae-aun" to mean to appease, without knowing that the essential meaning of the term is to "good cheek" someone. One of the advantages of the Anishinaubae language is that a speaker need not memorize all the words or have heard them all. He may need to memorize no more than a few hundred prefixes, suffixes, verbs and nouns, and yet he will have a vocabulary numbering thousands.

But more important than language itself was what the tribe, through its Elders, intended for its youth, and how best the tribe could prepare youth for the life abroad. Youth learned from the stories what to expect from life, what was good for the tribe, what for the individual.

It was clear that there needs to be order and control and discipline and some means of enforcing them, even in a small community. And the only means that the old tribesmen had of instilling in youth and in its members a sense of what ought to be done and what ought not to be done was through story, not only for the sake of harmony within the community, but for survival itself. The tribe had no means of enforcing its members to do what ought to be done except to instill in each person an intent to do what was best for the tribe, family and for self. And if a tribal member flouted tribal custom or code, he or she might suffer no more than ridicule and at worst retaliation at the hands of a fellow tribal member, or retribution at the hands of an evil manitou.

It was taken for granted that men and women generally meant well. Perhaps it is for this reason that our ancestors called themselves, and gave to our tribe, the name "Anishinaubaek", the good beings. But it is also in the nature of men and women that they cannot keep their minds on their intentions. They also discourage easily, but there are a hundred other reasons why men and women do not always fulfill their intentions or live up to their dreams and visions, or quite measure up to tribal expectations.

To represent this aspect of human nature, the tribe invented or dreamed into being Nana'b'oozoo. Nana'b'oozoo was full of good intentions. Nana'b'oozoo is a manitou, but even manitous, as our ancestors believed, were bound by human needs and passions, and by physical laws of the world. The instant that he hears of the abuse of his people by the Weendigo, Nana'b'oozoo leaves his home and village to avenge his tribal brothers and sisters. When he gets to the Weendigo's camp, Nana'b'oozoo dares the enemy warriors to battle, but on seeing the evil aspect of manitous and their number, runs in terror for his very life. With winter coming on, the tribe's stock of food would not carry the people through the winter, Nana'b'oozoo counselled rationing and sharing the meagre supply. But secretly Nana'b'oozoo had no intention of sharing his food. Later, all Nana'b'oozoo found was a pile of dried fungi where he had stored his own meats. For the rest of the winter, until the first berries ripened in the spring, Nana'b'oozoo was forced to eat dried berries that he found still clinging to the trees. Another time, Nana'b'oozoo was worried that his family would suffer during the coming winter. He therefore asked the heron how he managed to catch fish so easily. The heron told Nana'b'oozoo how to fish, but warned him not to take any more than he needed. Nana'b'oozoo fished, but he could not be content with one fish; he had to have more and more and more at that moment, not tomorrow. During the night all his fish turned into ice. Nana'b'oozoo concocted elaborate schemes to reduce the time and labour expended in hunting ducks. He wanted the entire flock, not just one. What better way was there than to steal upon them underwater, bind their legs together and then tow them to shore? But the moment that the ducks felt the tow-line, they took flight and bore Nana'b'oozoo into the skies. Nana'b'oozoo weakened, lost his hold and tumbled into a lake.

Nana'b'oozoo was dreamed into being, into the world of myth, and into the world of reality.

But Nana'b'oozoo is myth only insofar as he performed the fantastic and the unbelievable; otherwise he is real to the extent that he symbolizes mankind and womankind in all their aspirations and accomplishments, or in all their foibles and misadventures.

As men and women get to know something of human nature and the codes that regulate human conduct that are based on the understanding of human nature, they will also come to know tribal institutions and ideas and beliefs that bear upon tribal customs, government and society itself.

No more than a few examples need to be adduced to show what are some of these tribal institutions.

Take the matter of the notion of property. For the Anishinaubae tribe, ownership of land was conferred by Kitchi-Manitou upon the Nation, and for as long as the Nation endures, so long will it possess title and right to the land, and a claim to the yield of the land, air, and its waters. Only the Nation owned the land; only the tribe had a permanence commensurable with the existence of the land; the Nation is part of the land and cannot be regarded as separate from it. A person has only tenure and an ownership during the course of his life, and a trust to care for the land for the benefit of tribe and future generations, who in their turn will come into tenure and trust.

If there was little government, and if chiefs and their councillors who superintended the affairs of their communities had as their authority only their experience, knowledge, ability and character, there was little need for more government. Even if there was need for more government, as the Anishinaubaek and their neighbours, the Six Nations Peoples, implicitly recognized in their institution of the Council of Three Fires and in the League of Peace, they would have always preferred less; they had freedom and equality.

It is not likely that the Anishinaubaek or their Six Nations neighbours would have surrendered their personal freedom, or readily submitted to authority. Such was their conviction of their intrinsic worth and equality that the Anishinaubae peoples seldom deferred to naked authority or yielded their independence or entrusted their well-being to another except on special occasions, and only for brief periods. In Anishinaubae eyes, men and women were equal and free. To this day the Anishinaubae peoples' conviction in equality of worth remains as firm as it has always been, and their resentment of any intrusion upon their independence through the exercise of authority has not abated.

Action and wisdom and accountability were the stuff of men and women, chiefs and councillors. Next to deeds, what the Anishinaubaek most respected was speech. To the Anishinaubaek and other tribes, words were no less medicinal. They were medicine and sacred, bad and good; they could injure or heal, offend or comfort, mislead or enlighten. And insofar as words move or inform, they are the creations of the speaker, reflecting his or her moods, sentiments and skill with ideas. And just as the medicine man or woman can heal only as much as his or her limited powers allow, so a speaker can impart only what is within his knowledge, and articulate only what is within his command of language.

At best and at most, all that a speaker could attain or be expected to attain was the highest degree of accuracy in describing what was within his knowledge and experience. The person abiding by the principles of addressing only those matters within his knowledge, and describing as accurately as his vocabulary enabled him/her, was said to have spoken as far as he or she could cast his or her knowledge by means of words. And just as a medicine person administered his/her medicine only for the purpose intended, so a speaker took care to speak only about matters within his knowledge and experience. Of such a person people said, "w'daebawae", he/she speaks the truth. A person abusing the truth and language was ridiculed with "w'geewinimoh", he or she speaks in circles as a dog barks in circles in uncertainty.

In the course of learning language, much more than speech is received. In the study of language much more than the ability to utter words or to express simple wants and sentiments is expected. The end of language is to glean some understanding of the transcendental, the world, life, being, human nature, laws, physical and human-inspired as embodied in literature. Only in the context of literature does language make sense; and it is only in the ambit of literature that languages studies, courses and exercises find relevance.

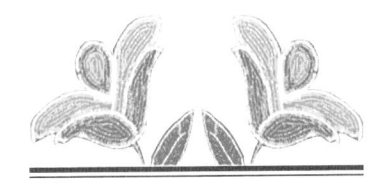

How Should Ojibway or Other Tribal Names be Spelled?

Basil H. Johnston, O.Ont., LLD., B.A. © May 1986

How Should Ojibway or Other Tribal Names be Spelled?

"What should be in that Caesar? Why should that name be sounded more than yours? Write them together; yours is as fair a name. Sound them, it doth become the mouth as well; weigh them, it is as heavy; conjure with them, Brutus will start a spirit as soon as Caesar." Such was the way by which Cassius tried to incite Brutus against Caesar, comparing the relative merits of names.

Now, by comparison with human names, geographic names may not be as heavy, but they may be as fair, become the mouth as well and even conjure up spirits and passions.

Is not Ontario as fair and as poetic as is New Brunswick? Quebec as is Newfoundland? Manitoba as is Nova Scotia? Saskatchewan as is New France? Mississauga as is Newcastle? Toronto as is New Liskeard? Winnipeg as is new Westminster? Niagara as is Newmarket? Nootka Sound as is New Waterford? "Write them together the Native is as fair a name. Sound them, they doth become the mouth as well."

Why should these names be sounded more than yours? New Hampshire, New Amsterdam, New York, New England, New Glasgow, New Acadia, New Albany, New Annan, Newark, New Boston, New Britain, New Canaan, New Canada, New Denmark, New Dublin, New Scotland, New France, New Germany, New Ireland, New Norway, New Prussia, New Zealand; and there are at least 170 more place names in Canada beginning with the affix "New."

Why should these names be sounded more than Inuvik, Pavungnituk, Ungava, Kasungatak, Whycocomagh, Wagamatcook, Antigonish, Merigomish, Shubenacadie, Chedabucto, Chignecto, Kejimkijik, Kennebecasis, Magaguadavic, Miramichi, Saguenay, Kenogami, Shawinigan, Madawaska, Maskinonge, Mississquoi, Caughnawaga, Mississippi, Maniwaki, Petawawa, Temiscaming, Chibouqamau, Matagami, Mistassini, Winisk, Mississagi, Couchiching, Abitibi, Muskoka, Niagara, Temagami, Penetanguishene, Oshawa, Gananoque? Write them together, they are as fair; sound them, somehow they do not become the mouth as well.

And I suspect that it is because they do not become the mouth as well in all speakers that they even conjured this Ontario Geographic Names Board Symposium.

What is it like with other languages or what other tribes and nations think about bringing the spellings of Native languages into line so Native words or geographic names become all mouths equally well, I know not. I can only speak from my tribal bias, and from my own prejudice and experience.

But I do not believe that my tribal brothers or sisters are as offended by the mispronunciation of our words as some people are anxious to utter our words and names as fluently as do the Native speakers. I have never heard a tribal brother or sister complain about or condemn non-Natives for their pronunciation. They may have condemned them for many other things, but not for mispronunciation. I have never heard a tribal brother or sister say "They are massacring our language; they are mangling our words; they are ruining Neebeeshing by saying Nipissing, Manitou-minissing by saying Manitoulin, Anim-beegoong by saying Nipigon, Assinee-bawaun by saying Assiniboine, Manitoubaung by saying Manitoba, Kizauski-idjiwiwinaung by saying Saskatchewan, Zigimay by saying Sakimay, Ochipawaehnce by saying Ochapowace, N'okomiss by saying Nokomiss; they should leave our language alone."

No! Until recently, members of our tribe have never criticized the pronunciation of our neighbours, brothers, sisters, cousins, or compatriots. They have not criticized the pronunciation of citizens of this country and the United States or European, African or Asiatic origin any more than they would criticize a child learning to speak his or her first words. For, far more important to them than sound was the attempt and the sense. For what difference does it make if a speaker were to utter "How do you do?" as a Chinese might, or an Italian, or a Frenchman, or an Englishman? In language, what is important is to understand and to give understanding, isn't it?

Now, if our words do not become all mouths equally well, it is because that it is only natural that men and women of whatever nationality will articulate all words of whatever origin according to the cadence, rhythm and accent and phonetics of their Native language. Give any word in my language and offer it for imitation to any person of European extraction and

THINK INDIAN

the Englishman may pronounce it with an Oxford accent, as a Scotsman in a Celtic, as a Frenchman may with Parisian style, as a Spaniard in Castilian, as a German may in Bavarian, as an Italian may in Genoese, as an Irishman may in brogue and as a Chinese may in Cantonese. It cannot be helped. A person cannot and ought not to be expected to pronounce a word in a language not his/her own in accents or inflections other than his own language or in cadence, rhythm or accent other than in terms of his training and experience. As one hears, so will one pronounce; as one pronounces, so will one spell.

Given this human predilection, it ought not evoke surprise then that there are at least eighteen different spellings for Ojibway. Now the word Ojibway is not the only word to suffer mutilation in the course of translation, transliteration and spelling. The names of individuals too have been maimed, some to a greater degree than others. For the families known as "Nothings," "Masons," and "Walkers" this is how it came about. During the issue of annuity monies in the north, the Indian Agent asked the Indian standing before him "What's your name?" The Indian replied "Nawautin." The Indian Agent wrote down "Nothing," forever altering the meaning and the sense embodied in Nawautin from "Serene" to "Nothing." But not only did the Agent inflict a meaningless name on the family, he also forced the members of that family to explain their surname many thousands of times over. In Saugeen the Indian Agent registering the names of the band conferred the name "Mason" on a family whose name was "Mazaun." With one flourish of the pen the Agent stroked the meaning of "Hawthorn" out of existence. Waukae-Geezhig was a common name that represented a large clan. As it was too pagan and too long for baptismal and academic records, some registrar cropped the name to Waukey. Still later the name "Waukey," not nearly enough Anglo-Saxon in complexion, was changed to Walker. But not all members of the clan chose the name Waukae or Waukey; some preferred to retain "Geezhig." Even this name underwent change, evolving into "Day." Despite all these changes and alterations, the name "Waukae-Geezhig" endures in the Wikwemikong on Manitoulin Island. When sound is allowed to be the governing factor in the spelling of words, then there can be no uniform spelling but almost as many variations as there are nationalities and dialects.

The early chroniclers did the same thing: they recorded place names according as they heard them and according as they had been trained in their phonetic system without knowing the customs of the people or the meanings of words. From their spellings, neither the sound nor the meaning is readily gleaned from Chicoutimiens, Papinachoise, Nemisco, Ouaouechkairini, Kichesiprini, Kotakoutouemi, Mataousharini, Nipisiriens, Ouasouarini, Baouichitigouiam. In order to adduce the pronunciation and the meaning of the words as spelled, the translator or transcriber must know the customs of the nationality of the writer as well as the spelling style of his language. As spelled, some place names have misled scholars in their fieldwork and have become issues in land claims hearings and litigation.

But sound and meaning are not the only factors governing orthography. Men and women love to abbreviate; they abbreviate titles, addresses and dresses with equal ease and indifference. Now abbreviation may bring about certain advantages and confer benefit in writing, but it has its risks and traps if it is done without regard for the changes in meaning that may result. Like other peoples, my tribe likes to abbreviate, and my tribal brothers and sisters can abbreviate with the best when they put their minds to it. Some years ago one of our tribal brothers was asked to name and to provide the spelling of the name of a vessel on the occasion of its launching. To help the White people pronounce the Indian name of the ship, our tribal brother exercised his prerogative of abbreviating the name of the vessel. In so doing he inadvertently rendered a spelling that was similar to another word in the language than meant "to urinate." Other tribal members familiar with orthography referred to the new vessel as the "Pee Pee Boat." There is a little town in Ontario somewhere which means "manure." Now it came by this name quite honestly. The White people found the name short, charming and easy enough to pronounce. They adopted the name for their town without knowing the meaning. Only a few Native people know the origin and meaning of the word and they have kept the secret to themselves. It's just as well. Otherwise the mayor of said "Town of Manure" would never again wear his chain of office. Fortunately, not all words or terms so abbreviated transform into or take on meanings that may be objectionable or ridiculous. Nevertheless, the two instances mentioned ought to serve as examples of what could possibly result if sound and ease of pronunciation are used as criteria for spelling.

Words that have little or no meaning can be chopped and altered in spelling without impairing the word or giving offence to the inhabitants, if the word happens to be the name of a place. It's no big deal. Scarborough remains Scarborough, even though "borough" has been amputated to "boro." The same is true of Peterborough. And has any public outcry been heard protesting the increased use of "The Soo" instead of Sault Ste. Marie? Has anyone objected to the gradual dissolution of Portage La Prairie and the installation of Portage? These are names and sounds that have simply been affixed to places mainly for sentimental reasons, I suspect, and as such can be shaped and reshaped. Take Newcastle, for instance: the name has been conferred upon this little town even though no castle, new or old, has ever been constructed there. It is just a name. And is there some feature, trait, building or institution in New Westminster, B.C. to justify the name? Certainly the name suggests that the "new" bears some likeness to the old in some respects. Or is New Westminster just a name and a sound like the rest?

What has been done to Scarboro and to Portage and what is being done to many other towns cannot be done to Native place names without destroying their essential meanings. Consider the fate of Minidauwingausheeng. It was recorded in history, geography and other books as Penetanguishene, and in more recent times the name meaning "the place of (a type of) sands, has been abbreviated to Penetang. As is, it becomes the mouth, but makes no sense. Zheebau-piko-idjiwun went through the same kind of amputation until it became "Bobcaygeon." It too becomes the mouth after a fashion, but not the essential sense. And what is Scugog now but a sound without meaning? Before it was shaved, chiselled and filed down into its present being it was Piyaugawaushaugaug, or was it Piyagawaeshicugog?

The reasons that brought about Penetang, Bobcaygeon and Scugog may well have been sensible, but this is not always the case. Caprice and whim sometimes bear and influence. Because of hockey, Wikwemikong is going through mutation, or is it mutilation? It is becoming increasingly fashionable to refer to that Reserve community as "Wiky" from the inscription on the sweaters of the two hockey teams, The Wiky T-Birds and the Wiky Buzzards. Generations from now no one may remember that Wiky was once Weequaed-amikoong, "The Bay of the Beavers." It will be just another name without meaning, altered and abbreviated for the sake of hockey.

To seek means by which to make pronunciation easier is not reason enough to institute a uniform spelling system, for just as abbreviation alters meaning, so will any spelling based only on sound. Native place names are not just sounds; they are full of meaning to the speakers of the language and the spelling, whatever the system, must reflect that meaning.

It is precisely because Native place names have meaning that we of this generation know something of our ancestors, of their customs, of their perceptions, of their relationships with one another and the land, and of their practice of naming places after some unique or distinct characteristic. Niagara, today regarded as a place of romance and a wonderful starting point for wedded bliss, was to the practical Tuscarora no more than a "bisected bottomland" which they might have spelled "Ongniaahra." "Ottawa" referred to the guardsmen of our ancestral territories. The word relates to their functions either to grant entry into Anishinaubae territory upon payment of a tariff or to turn visitors away. The term derives from "adauwae or adjauwae" which means to exchange. "Ontario," as the Mohawks observed, means fair, beautiful to behold. How much better and more suitable than Upper Canada or New Britain or some other monstrosity. Quebec came from "Gaebauc"—because the river appears to be closed or blocked by Diamond Cape from a certain perspective. Manitoba means the Land of the Manitou, from the Manitou nature of the straits connecting two large bodies of water. Native words are more than sound.

Besides abbreviation and spelling according to sound rather than meaning, there is another element that threatens to change the spelling of many words and render them meaningless sounds. Mississauga, I understand, is giving offence. It is a beautiful name in my language, meaning "wide river mouth," and is the name that my tribe gave to those members of our tribe who dwelt at the wide river mouth. As the name adopted by the municipality that is situated between Brampton, Etobicoke and Oakville, it is not particularly difficult to pronounce. Still it has been mangled, not a great deal perhaps, but enough. For years Mississauga was inscribed on maps, stationery and called out by bus drivers without once giving pain. Now all this has changed, I'm given to understand. Mississauga is giving offence not

THINK INDIAN

from its length, not from its meaning, but because it is sexist. The charge is that Mississauga embodies sexist and divisive and discriminatory elements. It is sexist in the sense that it singles out the unmarried and discriminates against those who prefer Mz. or Ms. and perpetuated unequal status. Then there were others who derived the term Mrs. from Mississauga and inferred that it preferred and upheld the married state of women in preference to spinsterhood.

Now suppose that Mississauga is indeed declared to be objectionable and is abusive to womenkind and their aspirations, and deserves to be guillotined. I imagine that a gang of linguists will be retained to undertake the surgery, provided they can agree which end to dissect and how much. It is most likely that "Missis" would be pruned, and if one "s" is retained, the new name will be Sauga, and if no "s" is kept, then the remainder will be Auga. And just as sure as Custer shouted "Where did all the Indians come from?" so will someone with a pronounced idiolect respecting the "R" will call the place Sauger or Auger; and the citizens will be known as Saugers or Augers. Now changing Mississauga to Sauga or to some other literary or linguistic freak would not be the end of it.

You see, the name does not refer only to a place or one place, it refers as well to people who may have more right to it than a municipality. Who ever initiates the change in the spelling of Mississauga to Sauga ought personally deliver notice to the Mississaugas of the New Credit and the Mississaugis of Mississaugi in Northern Ontario that, owing to the sexist and discriminatory character of their names, their names were changed, and that from then on they were to be known as Saugas or Saugers or Augas. The person delivering such notice of change of name is advised to commit to memory Custer's most memorable words, "Where in hell did all the Indians come from?" Of course, the same courier acting on behalf of the group or movement would have to persuade archeologists, anthropologists, ethnologists and publishers to alter all their texts.

Let us suppose further that Mississauga were stricken from all records and speech for being too sexist; what would become of Manitoba? Maniwaki? Mississippi? Manitoulin? Manitowaudae?

But upon such feeble grounds are decisions respecting many matters, including that of language, sometimes made.

Now to seek a uniform spelling in order to bring about uniform pronunciation may well constitute solid grounds, but that is no warranty that the sense or the meanings of Native words will be upheld, or is there any warranty that accurate pronunciation will be obtained.

Just as long as English pronunciation is in a state of uncertainty, English itself does not strictly conform to set standards in pronunciation, or users of the alphabet do not abide by the same phonetic systems, no uniformity can be brought to the pronunciation of "Indian words and names." If speakers of the English language cannot agree on the spelling of "mishi" but spell it with a "ch" as in Michigan, or with a double "s" as in Mississauga, or with a single "s" as in Muskellunge, or with a "c" as in Mickesaubee, how is a uniform spelling to be established for my tribal language, or that of any other tribal language?

When the English tongue we speak
Why is break not rhymed with freak?
Will you tell me why it's true
We say sew but likewise few?
And make of a verse
Cannot cap his horse with worse?
Beard sounds not the same as heard;
Cord is different from word;
Cow is cow, but low is low
Shoe is never rhymed with foe.
Think of hose and dose and lose,
And think of goose and yet choose.
Think of comb and tomb, and bomb
Doll and roll, and home and some
And since pay is rhymed with say
Why not paid with said I pray?
We have blood and food and good,
Mould is not pronounced like could.
Wherefore done, but gone and lone
Is there any reason known?
And in short, it seems to me
Sound and letters disagree.

(Anonymous)

THINK INDIAN

Instead of pressing for a uniform system in the spelling of Native place names as some provincial geographic names boards are doing, it would be better for them to follow the example of the Commission de Toponymie of the Province of Quebec in favouring "the names used by local Natives, when official names are being given." In addition, provincial names boards should follow local usage and practice in the spelling of names rather than some system devised in some place distantly removed from the feature to be named. While different spellings may result, they ought not be regarded necessarily as signs of disagreement or even illiteracy, rather different spellings will reflect different perceptions, different usages and different styles, and as such may be the means by which the inhabitants may be identified.

As Moloch said to his kindred devils, "You have what I advise."

THINK INDIAN

DO SOMETHING FOR YOUR PEOPLE

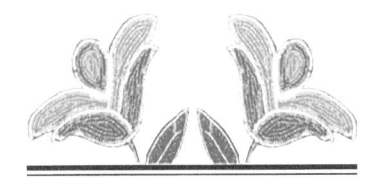

Basil H. Johnston, O.Ont., LLD., B.A. © June 1986

Do Something For Your People

In former days tribes counselled their youth to "Do something for your people," and they had their means and methods of training and instruction to prepare their youth to fulfill tribal obligations. What tribes expected of and counselled their youth in generations past still has application today. Though you can no longer make ready or serve your people in the old way, you must, if you are to help your people, take courses and programs, risks and opportunities that render you discerning in judgement, fit in body, and mindful of the well-being of your tribe.

Now, what is it that restrains our Native brothers and sisters from taking part in the world of commerce or business?

In addition to the anxieties and uncertainties caused by inexerience and unfamiliarity with the processes of establishing and operating a company, there is a fear that business, as have religion and education before, will be the means of assimilation. Precisely in what senses business would accomplish this has not been described, but the fear lingers like a gray cloud that will not go away.

There is fear that business will assimilate or hasten the assimilation of the tribes. There is a fear that business practices will corrupt the fundamental spirituality of the Indians, and there is fear that business is founded on traits too alien to Native Indian traditional and cultural values.

Is any one justified in thinking or believing that by becoming an accountant, a sales manager, an engineer, a real estate representative, an administrator, a bank manager, a marketing consultant, a marina operator, a grocery store proprietor will bleach one's pigmentation, or blanch one's ideas or way of thinking or perceiving things? I see little difference between what our ancestors did in accepting the West European technology and what the present generation and what other races have done in accepting West European and American techniques, systems and procedures.

When our ancestors saw the advantages of metal tools and weapons and textiles and ornaments, they put away their stone axes, bows and arrows, their loin-cloths, and took up the musket, the cast iron pot, the tempered axe, the steel knife; put on hats and lace, and adorned their coats and gowns and gauntlets with beads and bangles, and kept their languages, their values, their customs and their perspectives.

Really, instead of being apprehensive for your tribal identity, you should take heart in the experience of other peoples who have adopted technologies and techniques of yet other races. Few have made better use of West European and American technology and know-how than have the Japanese. Yet they remain as Japanese as before. And it is partly because they have adjusted to change and taken control of new technologies that the Jews have remained what they have ever wanted to be and what they are in spirit, as well as in outlook. And do not these examples illustrate that, instead of being an agent of assimilation, business may well be a means by which tribal and national identities are preserved.

And will the fundamental materialism of business or commerce corrupt the essential spirituality of the Indian peoples? Such fears or apprehensions as there are give some credence to the notion that the sole interest and purpose in life of entrepreneurs such as automobile dealers, stock-brokers, funeral directors, cosmetic manufacturers, lawyers, chemists, is to make a fortune, acquire all sorts of worldly goods, and to the devil with the rest of mankind. Now this approach to life may indeed be true of some men and women in industry, but it is not equally true of all.

There are business men and women whose interests go beyond the margin of balance sheets and further than the next Dow-Jones report, and extend into music, theatre, literature, art, religion, science and humanities and other spheres. The man or the woman with the briefcase may well attend As You Like It or a performance by the Toronto Symphony Orchestra. The owner of a large discount store also owns a theatre; the owner of Uranium Mines has provided money for the construction of churches; the President and Chairman of the Board of a large optical company served as Chairman of the Board of Trustees of the Royal Ontario Museum, and the Chairman of the Board of Shopper's Drug Mart is a Founding Chairman of the Canadian Council for Native Business. In not one of these instances is there evidence that an actor became less artistic, or a clergyman less pious, or an academic less scholarly, or that Indians became less tribal.

Judging from the experience of our ancestors and other peoples such as the Japanese in their association with businessmen of West-European origin or in the exercise of occidental business practices, there is nothing to fear.

And what is this spirituality of the Natives that must be protected against loss and nurtured into continuity? Precisely what is the meaning of the oft-repeated expression "the Native peoples are very spiritual?"

Now I do not know whether the term "spiritual" exactly describes that trait which is one of the distinctive characteristics of the Native peoples of this country and this continent. For my part I object to the use of the term, not only in its application but also for its connotation. From their beliefs and rituals and customs and practices I would prefer the term "reverential" as more aptly descriptive of the character of the Indians.

The reverence arose from the belief that there was in everything and everyone, rock, wind, mountain, lake, river, corn, melons, tobacco, nightshade, bloodroot, a hawk, eagle, turtle, sturgeon, man, woman, a little of the essence and substance of Kitchi-Manitou, the Great Mystery. According to this belief, every being was endowed with some of this mystery that deserved respect, reverence. In practice, this reverence was expressed in the form of rituals of thanksgiving performed upon the killing of game and the proper disposition of their bones, and the due conservation of pairs of animals for future needs and for future generations.

Two great concepts were generated by this tribal and individual reverence for life and being. In the first there evolved the notion that men and women were but trustees of the land and the waters and the skies, and co-tenants upon the land with the bear, the caribou, the beaver, the eagle, the hawk, the raven, the salmon, sturgeon, whitefish; and in the second there developed the notion that generations not yet born were entitled to the bounty and harvest of Mother Earth.

It would be a great loss for all, as the elders fear, for our people to surrender that reverence for the land, the waters, the skies, the winds, the manitous, and for other beings who share the earth with humankind, and to set aside that regard for the rights of unborn generations, and to adopt the attitude of the business and modern worlds that seem to say "strip the land, disembowel the earth, poison the stream, befoul the air. Take what you want, put nothing back. Tend to your own needs. You are not obligated to future generations; they can look after themselves."

But you need not give up this reverence for life or the regard for the needs of others in exchange for the materialistic outlook of business. Business, instead of being the means of changing your outlook, can be the means by which you can practice these tribal principles and perpetuate them.

Not only is business believed to represent an approach to life alien to that of the Native peoples, but it is also believed that success in business is grounded on personal traits.

It has been said that the Native peoples of this country have not the cultural or tribal tradition in competition, or acquisition or in abiding by clock governed schedules.

Now I do not know where these notions come from, how they got started, or how they came to be widely accepted as true. But there was competition. Boys and youths competed in foot-races, wrestling, swimming, stealth, imitation of birds and animals, marksmanship, weight-lifting, not for immediate rewards or recognition, but in preparation for the future. When they became men and women, they struggled with winds and blizzards, bears and whales and moose, and grappled with dreams and visions, tribal laws and individual impulses, not so much to defeat as not to be worsened. There was in our ancestors an urge to excel, to increase one's value through meeting challenges in the service of family and tribe.

And while it is true that, owing to the perishable nature of goods and the semi-nomadic character of life, our ancestors did not accumulate material possessions, our mythology abounds with stories of men and women desiring more than they needed. Much as they may have scorned selfishness and ungenerous men and women, and the storing up of goods, they toiled days through, in the camp and far abroad, in effort to store up enough smoked and dried fat, flesh and oil of animals, fish and birds, containers of corn, melons, beans, berries, maple sugar and nuts to sustain them from the first fall of snow until the earth yielded fruit again.

THINK INDIAN

The Indians of the interior would have laughed at their Pacific Coast brothers and sisters for their acquisitive spirit in massing boxes, loin-cloths, moccasins, cradle-boards, grave-markers, blankets, tools and copper. In turn, the Pacific Coast Indians might have regarded their interior brothers and sisters with contempt for their selfishness in having nothing to share with their neighbours.

Yet both would have been off the mark in their opinions of the others' values. For just as the Interior Indians would not have known that the Pacific Coast brethren and sister Natives were amassing worldly goods as a product of their industry and the fertility of the land and the sea, and to exercise their generosity in the distribution of goods, they would not have known that their Pacific Coast brothers and sisters had to renounce selfishness and to espouse selflessness in ritual. Neither would the Pacific Coast Indians have known that their brothers and sisters from the interior shared like views with them.

And because they didn't have clocks or calendars, it appeared that the Indian and the Inuit slept and waked, worked and rested, ate and played whenever they felt like it. "Indian time" people call it today. But Indian and Inuit were as punctual as the White men and women who awoke at 6:00 a.m., went to church at 7:00, ate at 8:00, commenced work at 8:30, ate again at 12:00 whether they were hungry or not, resumed work at 1:00, discontinued work at 6:00, ate at 6:30, began play at 7:00, and returned to bed at 9:00, with monotonous regularity, except that the Indian and the Inuit regulated their lives by the movement of the sun and the moon, the migrations of geese and caribou, the hibernation timetable of bears and other creatures who sleep the winter away, the ebb and flow of tides, the run and spawn of salmon, the flow of sap, the maturation of berries.

If the tribe wanted to eat and put away provisions for the winter, the hunters and fishermen and the berry pickers and the gardeners had to keep appointments with the herds of caribou and the schools of salmon, and the ripening of strawberries and the moment for planting, not when it suited their impulse or served their convenience.

Long before the caribou and the geese arrived the hunters were waiting, scanning the skies and straining their ears. Before the sap began to flow men and women and their children were there with spiles and buckets, waiting. Before the season for planting commenced the gardeners watched the phases of the moon for the signal to plant. Medicine men and women counted the days until the plants would ripen into full maturation.

These hunters and fishermen, gardeners and gatherers, healers and others were there waiting, not as they felt like it, but because nature's time had struck the hour and the day. There was no "Indian time" except for the very old and for the very young. Time did not and does not belong to the Indian; more properly it was caribou time, salmon time, maple sugar time, corn time which, though not as precise as solar time, the tribes had to follow. And that time extended from dawn until dusk, and thus long did the Indian work.

Though no one can say for certain when the caribou would arrive or the geese would be expected, or the sap would run, the Indians and the Inuit were already there waiting. They did not want to be late; they could not afford to be late. They well knew that the price for tardiness on the part of nature itself or on their part was starvation and hardship in the coming days of winter. And I imagine that had the caribou, the salmon, the sap and the corn all had followed a timetable, our ancestors would have been standing by, waiting.

Now the Indian may not be nearly as competitive as the Anglo-Saxon, or the Inuit not so punctual as Frenchmen, and neither may be as acquisitive as Americans, yet these traits are present in the Indian and the Inuit make-up to a sufficient degree to inspire some hope of success in business.

Our kin in Central and South America, endowed with no more competitive or promptness of spirit than our own ancestors, still managed to build cities and highways, water reservoirs and aqueducts, warehouses, depots and plazas, grew potatoes, maize, melons and beans, fabricated blankets and robes, sandals and shawls, made ornaments, vessels and utensils of gold and clay and common rock. And even though they had not the advantage of the wheel or a draft animal or metal tools, yet they produced sufficient goods to feed and clothe nations whose population numbered several millions, and still had surpluses for storage in depots.

THINK INDIAN

And though the Indian and Inuit people may not possess those traits deemed necessary for success in business, they do have other attributes that will serve them equally well, or even better.

Like all businessmen or entrepreneurs, the Indian and Inuit love and value their independence. They like to be in control of their lives and destinies, and there is hardly a sphere in the life of men and women better suited, or one that is more consistent with Native values than is the world of business for the exercise and the increase of individual independence. And Indians and Inuit share with businessmen and women a special regard for resourcefulness. What the tribe wanted in its members, and what every Indian and Inuit man and woman aspired for, was to have the confidence to declare "Give me the opportunity, give me a task and let me decide for myself how it is to be done. This I can do; this I have done."

So you see, business is not really alien to or at variance with Indian and Inuit traditions, dispositions, character, or aspirations. Not only is it not at odds with our purposes and interests, but it can be the very means by which you, the younger generation, can nurture your resourcefulness, gain greater independence, and enable you to carry out your tribe's mandate to "Do something for your people."

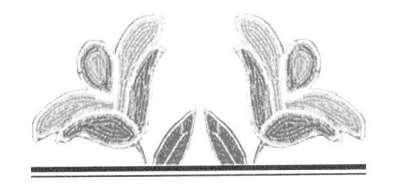

COWBOYS AND INDIANS

BASIL H. JOHNSTON, O. ONT., LLD., B.A. © 1987

THINK INDIAN

Cowboys and Indians

Hiring "real Indians" to take part in a movie involving Indians could only prove to be advantageous.
So thought the producer and director. It was not to be.

- told to me by Benjamin Pease

Hollywood grew fast and big. By the 1930's there were many studios employing many actors in the production of many motion pictures. Within the same few years, as the studios got bigger, techniques improved. As techniques improved, so did the quality of acting; and as acting got better, so did the range and variety of themes enlarge. And, of course, viewers' tastes became more refined and discriminating, requiring of Hollywood and the studios more authenticity in their productions.

And the studios were willing to oblige.

It was decided by the producer and director of a major studio planning a western picture, with either Hoot Gibson, Tom Mix or Ken Maynard as the principal star, to hire real Indians to take part in the production. With real Indians the advantages were obvious. Besides lending authenticity to the motion picture, Indians represented substantial savings. Their natural pigmentation would reduce expenses in cosmetics usually incurred in training greenhorns to ride; their possession of herds and ponies would save time and outlay in the rental and feeding of horses, and their natural talent for art would obviate the need for anthropologists to act as consultants in authenticating Indian art and design. The only expense to be incurred was the fee of $2.00 per day for movie extras.

Management calculated that 500 Indians, along with 500 horses, were needed for no more than two days to shoot an attack upon a wagon train. The producer and director also decided that there would be substantial savings by establishing the location of the filming near an Indian reservation somewhere in the west.

Inquiries, preliminary and cursory, made of historians and the Bureau of Indian Affairs in Washington indicated that the Crow Indians of Montana, having retained their traditions and still owning large herds of horses, would be best suited for a motion picture of the kind planned by the studio. Besides, the terrain in the area was genuine, honest-to-goodness Indian country, excellent for camera work.

Negotiations with the Bureau of Indian Affairs for permission to treat with the Crows for their services as actors, and for the provision of horses, began at once. Permission was granted by Washington, and the Crows were more than willing to take part.

Crew and cast arrived by train in Billings, Montana. Anxious to get started to finish shooting the siege of a wagon train in as short a time as possible, the producer and director sent a limousine to the reservation to fetch the chief.

Over a meal with the chief and his retinue of councilors and hangers-on, the producer, portly and bald beneath a cloud of smoke produced by a fat cigar, informed the chief that "it was a great privilege to work with the Crows, and that it was an honour and a distinction for his studio to set precedent in the entire industry by being the first to use real, live, honest-to-goodness Indians in a motion picture. For the Crows, it would mean fame and national recognition ... and money ... $2.00 per day for those taking part, $1.00 per day for those providing art work and the loan of teepees."

An interpreter translated for the chief.

The producer smiled and blew a cloud of smoke out of the side of his mouth. The Crow responded, "How! How! How!"

"It shouldn't take long chief, three or four days ... no more. A day to get ready, and two or three to film the scene. We don't want to interfere too much in your affairs; you've probably got a lot to do and ... we are working under a pretty tight schedule."

The interpreter relayed this information to the chief.

"Now chief, we want 500 warriors, 500 horses, bows and arrows and ... maybe fifty or so rifles ... feathers, head-dresses, buckskin jackets, and

… buckskin leggings … and four or five people who can paint designs on horses and put make-up on warriors." The producer continued, "The scene itself will be easy. The warriors will attack the wagon train at daybreak. It shouldn't take more than half an hour. Very easy; really don't need any rehearsals. My colleague will tell you what to do. Probably the easiest two bucks you'll ever make … cash, as soon as the scene's shot. Can you get all this stuff by tomorrow night, chief?" And the producer flicked ashes from his fat cigar.

The interpreter, prattling in Crow to his chief and councillors, pounded the table, slashed the air, shrugged his shoulders to emphasize his message to his listeners, who looked dumbfounded. Nevertheless, they injected a "How! How!" frequently enough into the discourse to intimate some understanding.

The chief said something.

"How many horses?"

"Five hundred; the producer might even settle for 450."

The interpreter addressed his chief, who shook his head, grunting "How!"

"Ain't got 500 horses," the interpreter said sadly.

"450?"

"Ain't dat many on de reservation."

"300?"

"No, not dat many, not like long time ago."

"Well! How many have you got?" the producer asked, his face pinching into worried lines and his voice losing its cheer and vitality.

"Maybe 10 … 20 … an' not very good dem."

"Keeee … rice!" And the producer bit a chunk of cigar, crushing the other end in the ashtray. "Are there any horses around here?"

"Yeah. Ranchers and farmers got dem."

To his assistant, the producer instructed, "Get 450-500 horses by tomorrow evening. We have to shoot that scene next morning with the Indians charging down the slope."

The interpreter whispered to his chief who shook his head.

"Say, mister," the interpreter addressed the producer, "how about saddles?"

"Saddles!" the word erupted.

"Yeah, saddles."

There was a moment of cosmic silence. "Saddles!" the producer repeated, mouthing the word in disbelief. "What do you mean ... saddles! You're all going to ride bare-back. This film is going to be authentic ... who ever heard of Indians riding on saddles ... supposed to be the finest horsemen in the world."

The interpreter stiffened in fright at the thought that he might be one of the warriors to ride bare-back, and he hung his head.

"Don't know how to ride ... us. Forget how ... long time ago ... need saddles ... might fall off an' git hurt ... us."

"This is incredible!... unbelievable! ... no horses! ... can't ride! ..." the producer gasped as he sank into the chair, "Keeeeee-rice."

Hope waning from his brow and voice, the producer tried, "You still got bows an' arrows?"

The interpreter slouched even lower. "No! Got none of dem t'ings, us."

"Buckskin outfits?"

"No." Another shameful shrug.

"Moccasins?"

"Some," a little brighter.

"Headdresses?"

"Maybe two, three—very old dem."

"Teepees?"

"No more—live in houses, us."

"Anyone know Indian designs ... you know—war paint for warriors ... and horses?"

"Don't t'ink so ... everybody forgot."

The producer groaned. "This is astounding ... I can't believe it.... No horses ... can't ride ... no teepees ... no buckskins ... no moccasins ... no ... no headdresses ... and ... probably not even loin-clothes..." and he was quivering. "It boggles the mind."

"What do we do?" the director asked.

After several moments, during which the producer assessed their circumstances, and possessing an analytical mind, he stated what needed to be done.

"With all our crew and cast here, and with our wagon-train and canon and horses, we can't very well go back now. We'll have to train these Indians to ride. Now ... Adams (the producer's assistant), I want you to get on the line right away. Get a guy who knows something about Indians, from the Bureau of Indians Affairs. I want you to get maybe a dozen chiefs' outfits, and 450-500 loin-cloths, bows an' arrows for everyone, about a dozen head-dresses and moccasins ... everything we need to make these Indians ... INDIANS. Is that clear? And get those horses by tomorrow night."

"Yes sir!"

"In the meantime, I'll call the studio office for more money. Let's get movin'."

The assistant went out.

"How long we gotta stay in this miserable God-forsaken cow-town?"

Ken Maynard inquired.

"Coupla weeks, maybe."

Ken Maynard groaned.

"Now!" directing his cigar at the interpreter and his remarks to the chief, the producer said, "Tell the chief to get 450-500 young men to learn to ride bare-back, an' to learn fast."

The interpreter apprised the chief of the message. The chief responded.

"He say $2.00 a day!"

"Keeee-rice! Tell him okay!"

Two mornings later, 500 horses, borrowed and rented from the local ranchers, were delivered to the Indian reservation. Five hundred Crows began practicing the art of horsemanship at once, and in earnest. And while it is true that many Crows shied away from horses, just as many horses shied away from the Crows, so that there was much anxious circling of horses around Indians and Indians around horses, pulling and jerking midst the clamour of pleas, "Whoa! Whoa! Steady dere Nellie! Easy dere!" all in Crow; and the horses, perhaps because they were unfamiliar with Crow, refused to "whoa." Eventually, horses and Crows overcame their mutual distrust and suspicions and animosities to enable the Indians to mount their beasts.

There were, of course, some casualties, a few broken legs, sprained ankles, cracked ribs and bruised behinds suffered by the novices on the first day, 50 in all. But by the third day, most of the young men, while not accomplished equestrians, were able to ride passably well; that is, they fell off their mounts less often.

With the arrival of the equipment, bows and arrows, head-dresses, moccasins, loin-cloths shipped by express from Washington, one day was set aside for the Crow warriors to practice shooting arrows from bows, first from a standing position, and then from horseback. There were a few more casualties, but nothing serious.

Along with the equipment came twelve make-up artists, accompanied by an anthropologist to advise the artists on war paint designs and to instruct the Crow in war-whooping. Twelve immense pavilions were erected; outside of each, billboards bearing symbols and markings representative of warrior war-paint and horse paint designs. Each Indian, having selected the design that best suited his taste and his horse, entered a pavilion where he or his steed were painted, emerging at the other end of the massive tent looking very fierce and ready for war.

The movie moguls decided that they would film the siege of the wagon-train at 5 a.m. regardless of the readiness of the Injuns. "So what if a few Redskins fall off their horses ... be more realistic."

As planned, and according to script, 10 Crows dressed in white buckskin, heavily beaded and wearing war-bonnets to represent leadership, along with 450 warriors wearing only loin-cloths and armed with bows and arrows, were assembled in a shallow depression unseen from the wagon-train. The horses pawed the ground and snorted and whinnied, while the director, producer, assorted assistants and cameramen, waited for the sun to cast its beams upon the wagon-train. When that critical moment occurred, signaled by an assistant with a wave of an arm, the directed shouted "Action! Cameras roll!"

Four hundred and fifty horses and riders erupted over the lip of the valley a hoopin' and a hollerin', their savage war-cries splitting the air, while 1800 hooves thundered down the slope, shaking the earth. Wagon train passengers spilled out of the covered-wagons, sprang up from blankets, seized rifles, yelling "Injuns! Injuns!" and hurled themselves behind boxes and crates and barrels and began firing. At one end of the valley Ken Maynard on his white charger waited for his cue; at the other end 50 cavalrymen to charge to the rescue. Bang! Bang! Bang! The Crows, a hoopin' an' a hollerin', were riding round and round the wagon-train, firing their arrows into the covered wagon and into boxes and crates and barrels. Bang! Bang! Bang! Round and round rode the Crows.

"Cut! Cut! Cut!" everyone was shouting. "Cut! Cut! Cut!" everyone was waving their arms. "Cut! Cut! Cut!" 450 Crows yelling "whoa! whoa! whoa! whoa!" brought their steeds to a halt.

THINK INDIAN

The Director, also on a horse, was livid with rage. He almost choked. "Somebody's gotta die; when you're shot, you fall off your horses and die. Don't you understand?"

The Indians nodded and grunted, "How! How!"

The Director, in disgust, rode off, leaving the cast and crew to repair 3000 to 4000 punctures and perforations inflicted by arrows on the canvas of the covered wagons. Six members of the cast, suffering injuries from stray arrows, needed medical attention. The Indians, with the arrows that they had recovered, retired to the reservation to mend their weapons.

Just before sun-up there was a final admonition. "Get it done right this time!" The warriors responded, "How! How!"

At the hand signal, "Action! Cameras roll!" were uttered.

Four hundred and fifty Indians on 450 horses boiled over the lip of the valley, a hoopin' an' a hollerin', their savage war-cries rending the peace, while 1800 hooves pounded down the slope, convulsing the ground. Wagon train patrons scurried out of covered wagons, sprang from blankets, seized their rifles, yelling "Injuns! Injuns!" and dove behind boxes and crates and barrels and began firing. Bang! Bang! Bang!

Seventy-five of the Crows, a hoopin' an' a hollerin', fell off their horses. Bang! Bang! Bang! Two hundred more Crows, a hoopin' an' a hollerin', spun off their mounts. Bang! Bang! Bang! The rest pitched off their steeds, who fled in all directions.

"Cut! Cut! Cut!" everyone was shouting. Four hundred and fifty Crows suspended their moanin' an' a groanin' an' a rollin' on the ground, even though many had sustained real injuries, to listen to and to watch the director.

There was a torrent of curses, sulphuric glares which eventually subsided into mutterings, the gist of which was relayed by the interpreter to the chiefs and warriors "that not everyone should have fallen off his horse." To this the chief replied, "$2.00."

The scene was re-enacted the next day without incident. After the shooting there were handshakes all around, and expressions of admiration tendered by Ken Maynard to the Crows for the speed with which they had developed horsemanship, remarking that "it must be in-bred."

Crew and cast were celebrating over wine and whiskey, cheese and crackers when the film editor summoned the Director. "Come here and look at these," he said., thrusting a magnifying glass to his superior. The Director held the film strip against the light; he applied the magnifying glass to the stills.

"Sun-glasses! Keeee-rice ... sun-glasses ... those damned Indians. Keeee-rice ... what next? ..."

When told, the producer kicked a chair after hurling a bottle into a corner; for close to 10 minutes he cursed Indians. But it was useless, the scene had to be shot again.

Horses and Indians had to be recalled and re-assembled for retakes, for which the good chief demanded $2.00 for his people. It took another week before the wagon-train siege was filmed to the satisfaction of the producer and his director. In the interim there were two days of rain, one filming aborted by several Crows wearing watches, an extra filming of a prairie fire ignited by Ken Maynard that miscarried because several Crow warriors, supposedly dead, moved to avoid getting burned during a critical segment of the filming. When the first real epic of Cowboys and Indians was finally done, the Crows were jubilant, indebted to their chief for the prosperity and lasting renown that he exacted during difficult times. The producer and director, cast and crew departed in disquiet over having exceeded their budget.

Is That All There Is?
Tribal Literature

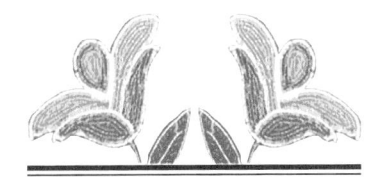

Basil H. Johnston, O.Ont., LLD., B.A. © 1989

Is That All There Is?

Tribal Literature

In the early 60's Kahn-Tineta Horn, a young Mohawk model, got the attention of the Canadian press (media) not only by her beauty but by her articulation of Indian grievances and her demands for justice. Soon after, Red Power was organized, threatening to use force. Academics and scholars, anxious and curious to know what provoked the Indians, organized a series of conferences and teach-ins to explore the issues. Even children wanted to know. So for their enlightenment experts wrote dozens of books. Universities and colleges began Native Studies courses. Ministries of Education, advised by a battery of consultants, adjusted their Curriculum Guidelines to allow units of study on the Native peoples of this continent. And school projects were conducted for the benefit of children between 10 and 13 years of age.

One such project at the Churchill Avenue Public School in North York, Ontario lasted six weeks, and the staff and students who had taken part mounted a display as a grand finale to their studies. And a fine display it was in the school's library.

In front of a canvas tent that looked like a teepee stood a grim chief, face painted in war-like colours and arms folded. On his head he wore a head-dress made of construction paper. A label pinned to his vest bore the name Blackfoot. I made straight for the chief.

"How!" I greeted the chief, holding up my hand at the same time as a gesture of friendship.

Instead of returning the greeting, the chief looked at me quizzically.

"How come you look so unhappy?" I asked him.

"Sir! I'm bored," the chief replied.

"How so chief?"

"Sir, don't tell anybody, but I'm bored. I'm tired of Indians. That's all we've studied for six weeks. I thought they'd be interesting when we started, because I always thought that Indians were neat. At the start of the course we had to choose to do a special project, from food preparation, transportation, dwellings, social organization, clothing, and hunting and fishing. I chose dwellings" and here the chief exhaled in exasperation, "… and that's all me and my team studied for six weeks; teepees, wigwams, longhouses, igloos. We read books, encyclopedias, went to the library to do research, looked at pictures, drew pictures. Then we had to make one. Sir, I'm bored."

"Didn't you learn anything else about Indians, chief?"

"No sir, there was nothing else … Sir? … Is that all there is to Indians?"

Little has changed since that evening in 1968. Books still present Native peoples in terms of their physical existence, as if Indians were incapable of meditating upon or grasping the abstract. Courses of study in the public school system, without other sources of information, had to adhere to the format, pattern and content set down in books. Students studied Kaw-ligas, wooden Indians, who were incapable of love or laughter; or Tontos, if you will, whose sole skill was to make fires and to perform other servile duties for the Lone Ranger, an inarticulate Tonto, his speech limited to "Ugh! Kemo Sabe Sabi," and "How."

Despite all the research and the field work conducted by anthropologists, ethnologists and linguists, Indians remain "The Unknown Peoples" as Professor George E. Tait of the University of Toronto so aptly titled his book written in 1973.

Not even Indian Affairs of Canada, with its more than two centuries of experience with Natives, with its array of experts and consultants, with its unlimited funds, seems to have learned anything about its constituents, if we are to assess their publication titled "The Canadian Indian." One would think that the Honourable William McKnight, then Minister of Indian and Northern Affairs, under whose authority the book was published in 1986, should know by now the Indians who often come to Ottawa do not arrive on horseback, do not slay one of the R.C.M.P. mounts and cook it on the steps of the Parliament buildings. Moreover, most Indians he has seen and met were not dressed in loincloths, nor did they sleep in teepees. Yet he authorized the publication of a book bereft of any originality or imagination, a book that perpetuated the notion and the image that the Indians had not advanced one step since contact but are still living as they had 150, even 300 years ago. There was not a word about Native thought, literature, institutions, contributions in music, art, theatre. But that's to be expected of Indian Affairs; to know next to nothing of their constituents.

Where did the author or authors of this latest publication by Indian Affairs get their information? The selected readings listed at the back of the book provide a clue: Frances Densmore, Harold Driver, Philip Drucker, Frederick W. Hodge, Diamond Jeness, Reginald and Gladys Laubin, Frank G. Speck, Bruce G. Trigger, George Woodcock, Harold Innis, Calvin Martin, E. Palmer Patterson, eminent scholars, none of whom spoke or attempted to learn the language of any of the Indian nations about whom they were writing. Modern scholars, because they are not required by their universities to learn, are no more proficient in a Native language than were their predecessors.

Herein, I submit, is the nub and the rub. Without the benefit of knowing the language of the Indian nation that they are investigating, scholars can never get into their mind the heart and soul and the spirit and still understand the Native's perceptions and interpretations. The scholar must confine his research and studies to the material, physical culture, subsistence patterns and family relationships.

Without knowing the spiritual and the intellectual, aesthetic side of Indian culture, the scholar cannot furnish what that little grade five youngster and others like him wanted to know about Indians.

Admitting his boredom was that grade five youngster's way of expressing his disappointment with the substance of the course that he and his colleagues had been made to endure. In another sense, it was a plea for other knowledge that would quench his curiosity and challenge his intellect.

Students such as he, as well as adults, are interested in the character, intellect, soul, spirit, heart of people of other races and cultures. They want to know what other people believe in, what they understand, what they expect and hope for in this life and in the next, how they keep law and order and harmony within the family and community, how and why these celebrated ceremonies, what made them proud, ashamed, what made them happy, what sad. Whether the young understand what they want to know and learn does not matter much, they still want to know in order to enrich their own insights and broaden their outlooks.

But unless scholars and writers know the literature of the peoples that they are studying or writing about, they cannot provide what their students and readers are seeking and deserving of.

There is, fortunately, enough literature, both oral and written, available for scholarly study, but it has for the most part been neglected. Myths, legends and songs have not been regenerated and set in modern terms to earn immortalization in poetry, dramatization in plays, or romanticization in novels.

What has prevented the acceptance of Indian literature as a serious and legitimate expression of Native thought and experience has been indifferent and inferior translation, a lack of understanding and interest in the culture, and a notion that it has little of importance to offer to the larger White culture.

In offering you a brief sketch, no more than a glimpse as it were, of my tribe's culture, I am doing no more than what anyone of you would do were you to be asked, "What is your culture? Would you explain it?" I would expect you to reply, "Read my literature and you will get to know something of my thoughts, my convictions, my aspirations, my feelings, sentiments, expectations, whatever I cherish or abominate."

First let me offer you an observation about my language for the simple reason that language and literature are inseparable, though they are too often taught as separate entities. They belong together.

In my tribal language all words have three levels of meaning; there is the surface meaning that everyone instantly understands. Beneath this meaning is a more fundamental meaning derived from the prefixes and their combinations with other terms. Underlying both is the philosophical meaning.

THINK INDIAN

Take the word "Anishinaubae". That is what the members of the nation, now known as Chippewa in the United States, or Ojibway in Canada, called themselves. It referred to a member of the tribe. It was given to the question "What are you?" But it was more than just a term of identification. It meant "I am a person of good intent, a person of worth", and it reflected what the people thought of themselves and of human nature, that all humans are essentially, fundamentally good. Let's separate that one word into its two terms. The first "Onishishih", meaning good, fine, beautiful, excellent, and the second "naubae", meaning being, human being, male, human species. Even together they do not yield the meaning "good intention." It is only by examining the stories of Nanabush, the tribe's central and principal mythical figure who represents all men and all women, that the term Anishinaubae begins to make sense. Nanabush was always full of good intentions, ergo the people of the tribe. The Anishinaubae perceive themselves as people who intended good and therefore of merit and worth. From this perception they drew a strong sense of pride, as well as a firm sense of place in the community. This influenced their notion of independence.

Let's take another word, the word for truth. When we say "w'daeb-awae" we mean he or she is telling the truth, is correct, is right. But the expression is not merely an affirmation of a speaker's veracity. It is as well a philosophical proposition that in saying a speaker casts his words and his voice as far as his perception and his vocabulary will enable him or her, it is a denial that there is such a thing as absolute truth; that the best and the most the speaker can achieve, and a listener expect, is the highest degree of accuracy. Somehow that one expression, "w'daeb-awae," sets the limits to a single statement, as well as setting limits to truth and the scope and exercise of speech.

One other word "to know." We say "w'kikaendaun" to convey the idea that he or she "knows." Without going into the etymological derivations, suffice it to say that when the speaker assures someone that he knows it, that person is saying that the notion, image, idea, fact that that person has in mind corresponds and is similar to what he or she has already seen, heard, touched, tasted or smelled. That person's knowledge may not be exact, but similar to that which has been instilled and impressed in his or her mind and recalled from memory.

The stories that make up our tribal literature are no different from the words in our language. Both have many meanings and applications, as well as bearing tribal perceptions, values and outlooks.

Let us begin at the beginning with the tribe's story of creation which precedes all other stories in the natural order. Creation stories provide insights into what races and nations understand of human nature; ours is no different in this respect.

This is our creation story. Kitchi-manitou beheld a vision. From this vision The Great Mystery, for that is the essential and fundamental meaning of Kitchi-manitou, and not spirit as is often understood, created the sun and the stars, the land and the waters, and all the creatures and beings, seen and unseen, that inhabit the earth, the seas and the skies. The creation was desolated by a flood. Only the manitous, creatures and beings who dwelt in the waters, were spared. All others perished.

In the heavens dwelt a manitou, Geezhigo-quae (Sky-woman). During the cataclysm upon the earth, Geezhigo-quae became pregnant. The creatures adrift upon the seas prevailed upon the giant turtle to offer his back as a haven for Geezhigo-quae. They then invited her to come down.

Resting on the giant turtle's back, Geezhigo-quae asked for soil.

One after another water creatures dove into the depths to retrieve a morsel of soil. Not one returned with a particle of soil. They all offered an excuse: too deep, too dark, too cold, there are evil manitous keeping watch. Last to descend was the muskrat. He returned with a small knot of earth.

With the particle of mud retrieved by the muskrat Geezhigo-quae recreated an island and the world as we know it. On the island she created over the giant turtle's shell, Geezhigo-quae gave birth to twins who begot the tribe called the Anishinaubaek.

Millennia later the tribe dreamed Nanabush into being. Nanabush represented themselves and what they understood of human nature. One day his world too was flooded. Like Geezhigo-quae, Nanabush recreated his world from a morsel of soil retrieved from the depths of the sea.

As a factual account of the origin of the world and of being, the story has no more basis than the biblical story of creation and the flood. But the story represents a belief in God, the creator, a Kitchi-manitou, the Great Mystery. It also represents a belief that Kitchi-manitou sought within himself, his own being, a vision. Or perhaps it came from within his being and that Kitchi-manitou created what was beheld, and set it into motion. Even the lesser manitous, such as Geezhigo-quae and Nanabush, must seek a morsel of soil with which to create and recreate their world, their spheres. So men and women must seek within themselves the talent or the potential and afterward create their own worlds and their own spheres and a purpose to give meaning to their lives.

The people begotten by Geezhigo-quae on that mythological island called themselves Anishinaubaek, the good beings who meant well and were human beings, therefore fundamentally good. But they also knew that men and women were often deflected from fulfilling their good intentions, and prevented from living up to their dreams and visions, not out of any inherent evil, but rather from something outside of themselves. Nanabush also represented this aspect of human nature. Many times Nanabush or the Anishinaubaek failed to carry out a noble purpose. Despite this, he is not rendered evil or wicked, but remains fundamentally and essentially good.

Men and women intend what is good, but they forget. The story called "The Man, The Snake and The Fox" exemplifies this aspect of human nature.

In its abbreviated form the story is as follows. The hunter leaves his lodge and his family at daybreak to go in search of game to feed his wife and his children. As he proceeds through the forest, the hunter sees deer, but each time they are out of range of his weapon.

Late in the afternoon, discouraged and weary, he hears faint cries in the distance. Forgetting his low spirits and fatigue he sets out with renewed optimism and vigour in the direction of the cries. Yet the nearer he draws to the source of the cries, the more daunted is the hunter by the dreadful screams. Only the thought of his family's needs drove him forward, otherwise he might have turned away.

At last he came to a glade. The screams came from a thicket on the opposite side. The hunter, bow and arrow drawn and ready, made his way forward cautiously.

To his horror the hunter saw an immense serpent tangled fast in a thicket as a fish is caught in the webbing of a net. The monster writhed and roared and twisted. He struggled to break free.

The man recoiled in horror. Before he could back away the snake saw him.

"Friend!" the snake addressed the man.

The man fell in a heap on the ground the moment that the snake spoke. When he came to much later, the snake pleaded with the man to set him free. For some time the man refused but eventually he relented. He was persuaded by the monster's plea that he too, though a serpent, had no less right to life than did the man. And the serpent promised not to injure the man on his release. The hunter was convinced.

The snake sprang on his deliverer the moment the last vine was cut away.

It was like thunder as the man and the snake struggled. Nearby a little fox heard the uproar. Never having seen such a spectacle the fox settled down to watch. Immediately he realized that the man was about to be killed.

Why were the snake and the man locked in mortal struggle? The little fox shouted for an explanation. The man and the snake stopped.

The hunter gasped out his story, then the snake gave his version. Pretending not to understand the snake's explanation, the fox beguiled the aggressor into returning to the thicket to act out his side of the story.

The snake entangled himself once more.

Realizing that he had been delivered from the edge of death by the fox, the man was greatly moved. He felt bound to show his gratitude in some tangible way. The fox assured him that no requital was required. Nevertheless the hunter persisted. How might he, the hunter, perform some favour on behalf of the fox?

Not only was there no need, the fox explained, there was nothing that the man could do for the fox; there was not a thing that the fox needed or desired of human beings. However, if it would make the man happier, the fox suggested that the man might feed him should he ever have need.

Nothing would please the man more than to perform some good for his deliverer; it was the least that he could do for a friend who had done so much.

Some years later the hunter shot a little fox who had been helping himself to the family storage. As the man drew his knife to finish off the thief, the little fox gasped, "Don't you remember?"

That no snakes as monstrous as the one in the story are to be found on this continent makes no difference to the youngsters' sense of outrage over the treachery of the snake and the forgetfulness of the man; nor does the exercise of speech which enables the snake and the fox to communicate with the hunter and each other prevent the young from being moved to compassion for the fox. Their sense of justice and fairness bears them over the anomalies in the story.

Before the last words "Don't you remember?" have echoed away, the young begin to ask questions. "Why? Why did the man not recognize the fox? Why did he forget? How did the man feel afterwards? Why did the snake attack the man? Why did the snake break his promise? Why didn't the man leave the snake where he was? Do animals really have as much right to live as human beings do?"

Indians cared, loved as passionately as other people.

The story called "The Weeping Pine" raises the same questions about love and marriage and the span of either that have been asked by philosophers, poets and lovers of every race and generation. It does not pretend to give answers to these age old questions beyond suggesting that love may bloom even in circumstances where it is least expected to flower and endure. But owing to shoddy translation, the story has been presented as an explanation for the origin of pine trees.

According to the story the elders of a village came to a certain young woman's home where she lived with her parents, brothers and sisters. They had come to let her family know that they had chosen her to be the new wife to an old man. This particular man had been without a friend since the death of his first wife some years before. The old man was described as good-natured and kind. As one who had done much to benefit the tribe in his youth, the old man deserved something in return from his neighbours. In the opinion of the elders the most fitting reward the old man could have was a wife. In their judgement the young woman they had chosen would be a suitable companion for the old man.

Because this sort of marriage was a matter that the young woman had not considered, it was unexpected. The delegation understood this. They did not demand an immediate answer but allowed the young woman a few days in which to make up her mind.

The young woman cried when the delegation left. She didn't want to marry that man. That old man whose days were all but over, and who could never look after her. She had, like every young girl her age, hoped to marry someone young, full of promise, someone she would love and who would love her in return. Besides, it was too soon. How could she, not yet eighteen, be a companion to an old man of seventy or more. The disparity was too great.

At first her parents too were aggrieved. But soon after they prevailed upon her to defer to the wishes of the elders, and her father delivered word of their daughter's consent to the elders.

But neither the disparity in age nor the disposition of the young girl to enter into a loveless marriage were too great; in the years that followed she came to love this old man. And they had many children.

Thirty years later the old man died.

On the final day of the four-day watch the mourners went home, but the widow made no move to rise. She continued to keen and rock back and forth in great sorrow.

"Come mother, let us go home" her children urged, offering to assist her to her feet and to support her on their way home.

"No! No! Leave me. Go" she said.

"Mother! Please. Come home with us," her children pleaded. Nothing they said could persuade their mother to leave.

"No. You go home. This is where I belong. Leave me."

Her children prayed she would relent; give in to the cold and hunger. They went home, but they did not leave their mother alone. During the next few days a son or daughter was always at her side, watching with her and entreating her to come home. They tried to comfort her with their own love and care, assuring her that her wound would pass and heal. They even brought her food and drink to sustain her. She refused everything.

As their mother grew weaker with each passing day, the children besought the elders to intercede on their behalf. Perhaps the elders could prevail on their mother.

But the elders shook their heads and said, "If that is what she wants, there is nothing that you can do to change her mind. Leave her be. She wants to be with him. Leave her. It's better that way."

And so the family ceased to press their mother to come home, though they still kept watch with her. They watched until she too died by the graveside of her husband, their father.

Using the term "grandchild" that all elders used in referring to the young, the elder who presided over the woman's wake said, "Our granddaughter's love did not cease with death, but continues into the next life."

The next spring a small plant grew out of the grave of the woman. Many years later as the sons and daughters and grandchildren gathered at the graveside of their parents, they felt a mist fall upon their faces and their arms. "It is mother shedding tears of love for dad," cried he daughter.

And it is so. On certain days spruces and pines shed a mist of tears of love.

By remaining at her husband's graveside until she too died, the woman fulfilled the implied promise "whither thou goest, there too will I go" contained in the term "weedjeewaugun," companion in life, our word for spouse.

As she wept for her love she must have wept for the love of her children. Their love threatened to break that bond that held her to her husband. No! She would not sever that bond; she would not let even death part her from the man to whom she had given her heart, her soul, her spirit forever.

It is unlikely that the woman ever uttered more than "K'zaugin" (I love you) during her marriage. In this respect she was no different from most other women, or men for that matter, who are not endowed with the poetic gift, though they feel and love with equal passion and depth. K'zaugin said everything. I love you today, tomorrow, forever. It expressed everything that the finest poets ever wrote and everything that the unpoetic ever thought and felt but could not put into rhyme or rhythm.

In sentiment the story compares to Elizabeth Barret Browning's immortal poem, "How do I love Thee" which ends with the words "and if God grant, I shall love thee better after death."

THINK INDIAN

ONE GENERATION FROM EXTINCTION

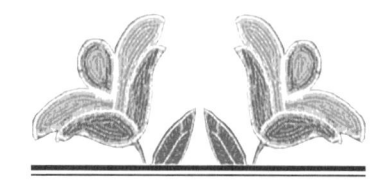

BASIL H. JOHNSTON, O.ONT., LLD., B.A. © DECEMBER 1989

ORIGINALLY PUBLISHED IN *CANADIAN LITERATURE*, VOL. 124-5, VANCOUVER, BC, 1990.

One Generation From Extinction

Within the past two years Gregor Keeshig, Henry Johnston, Racine Akiwenzie, Norman McLeod, Belva Pitwaniquot, died. They all spoke their Anishinaubae (Ojibway) language. When these elders passed away so did a portion of the Anishinaubae language come to an end as a tree disintegrates by degrees and in stages until it is no more; and, though infants were born to replenish the loss of life, not any one of them will learn the language of their grandfathers or grandmothers to keep it alive and to pass it on to their descendants. Thus language dies.

In some communities there are no more Gregor Keeshigs, Henry Johnstons, Racine Akiwenzies, Norman McLeods, Belva Pitwaniquots; those remaining have no more affinity to their ancestral language than they do Swahili or Sanskrit; in other communities the

languages may not survive beyond a generation. Some tribal languages are at the edge of extinction, not expected to survive for more than a few years. There remain but three aboriginal languages out of the original 53 found in Canada that may survive several more generations.

There is cause to lament, but it is the Native peoples who have the most cause to lament the passing of their languages. They lose not only the ability to express the simplest of daily sentiments and needs, but they can no longer understand the ideas, concepts, attitudes and rituals brought into being by their ancestors; and, having lost the power to understand, cannot sustain, enrich, or pass on their heritage. No longer will they think Indian or feel Indian. And though they may wear "Indian" jewellery or take part in powwows, they can never capture that kinship with or the reverence for the sun and the moon, the sky and the water, or feel the life beat of Mother Earth or sense the change in her moods; no longer are the wolf and the bear and the caribou elder brothers, but beasts, resources to be killed and sold. They will have lost their identity, which no amount of reading can ever restore. Only language and literature can restore the "Indianness".

Now, if Canadians of West-European or other origin have less cause than "Indians" to lament the passing of tribal languages it is because they may not realize that there is more to North American Indian languages than "ugh" or "how" or "kimu sabi." At most and at best, Euro-Canadians might have read or heard about Raven and Nana'b'oozoo and Thunderbirds and other "tricksters"; some may even have studied "Culture Myths," "Hero Tales," "Transformation Tales," or "Nature Myths and Beast Fables," but these accounts were never regarded as bearing any more sense than "Little Red Riding Hood" or "The Three Little Pigs." Neither language nor literature were ever considered in their natural kinship, which is the only way in which language ought to be considered if its range, depth, force and beauty are to be appreciated.

Perhaps our Canadian compatriots of West European origin have more cause to lament the passing of an Indian language than they realize or care to admit. Scholars mourn that there is no one who can speak the Huron language and thus assist scholars in their pursuit of further knowledge about the tribe; scholars mourn that had the Beothuk language survived, so much more would be known about the Beothuk peoples. In mourning the extinction of the language, scholars are implicitly declaring that the knowledge derived from a study of snowshoes, shards, arrowheads, old pipes, shrunken heads and old bones; hunting, fishing, transportation, food preparation, ornamentation, and sometimes ritual is limited. And so it is; material culture can yield only so much.

Language is crucial. If scholars are to increase their knowledge, and if they are to add depth and width to their studies, they must study a Native language and literature. It is not enough to know linguistics, or to know a few words or even some phrases, or to have access to the *Jesuit Relations, Chippewa Exercises, Ojibwa Texts,* or a *Dictionary of the Otchipwe Language*. Without knowledge of the language, scholars can never take for granted the accuracy of an interpretation or translation of a passage, let alone a single word; nor can they presume that their theses bear the kind of accuracy that scholarship and integrity demand. They would continue to labour under the impression that the word "manitou" means spirit, and that it has no other meaning. Superstitious nonsense, according to the White men. They do not know that the word "manitou" bears other meanings even more fundamental than "spirit," such as and/or pertaining to the deities; of a substance, character, nature, essence, quiddity, beyond comprehension, and therefore beyond explanation, a mystery, supernatural, potency, potential. What a difference such knowledge might have made in the studies conducted by Ruth Landes or Thomas B. Leekley and others on the Anishinaubae people. Perhaps … instead of regarding "Indians" as superstitious for positing "spirits" in trees or in other inanimate or insensate objects, they might have credited them with insight for having perceived a vital substance or essence that imparted life, form, growth, healing and strength in all things, beings, and places. They might have understood that the expression "manitouwun" meant that an object possessed or was infused with an element or a feature that was beyond human ken; they might have understood that "w'manitouwih" meant that he or she was endowed with extraordinary talents, and that it did not mean that he or she was a spirit.

Language is essential. If scholars and writers are to know how "Indians" perceive and regard certain ideas, they must study an "Indian" language. When an "Anishinaubae" says that someone is telling the truth, he says "W'daeb-awae." But the expression is not just a mere confirmation of a speaker's veracity. It is at the same time a philosophical proposition that in saying a speaker casts his words and his voice only as far as his vocabulary and his perception will enable him, the tribe was denying that there was absolute truth; that the best a speaker could achieve and a listener could expect was the highest degree of accuracy. Somehow that one expression, "w'daeb-awae," set the limits of a single statement, as well as setting limits on all speech.

There was a special regard, almost akin to reverence, for speech and for the truth. Perhaps it was because words bear the tone of the speaker, and may therefore be regarded as belonging to that person; perhaps it is because words have but a fleeting momentary existence in sound and are gone except in memory; perhaps it is because words have not ceased to exist but survive in echo and continue on into infinity; perhaps it is because words are medicine that can heal or injure; perhaps it is because words possess an element of the manitou that enabled them to conjure images and ideas out of nothing, and are the means by which the "autissokaunuk" (muses) inspired men and women. It was not without reason that the older generation did not solicit the "autissokaunuk" to assist in the genesis of stories or in the composition of chants in seasons other than winter.

THINK INDIAN

To instill respect for language, the old counselled youth "don't talk too much" (Kegoh zaum-doongaen), for they saw a kinship between language and truth. The expression is not without its facetious aspect, but in its broader application it was intended to convey to youth other notions implicit in the expression "Don't talk too much," for the injunction also meant "Don't talk too often ... don't talk too long ... don't talk about those matters that you know nothing about." Were a person to restrict his discourse and measure his speech and govern his talk by what he knew, he would earn the trust and respect of his (her) listeners. Of that man or woman they would say "w'daeb-awae." Better still, people would want to hear the speaker again, and by so doing bestow upon the speaker the opportunity to speak, for ultimately it is that people who confer the right of speech by their audience.

Language is a precious heritage; literature no less precious. So precious did the tribe regard language, speech, that it held those who abused language and speech and truth in contempt and ridicule, and withheld from them their trust and confidence. To the tribe, the man or woman who rambled on and on, or who let his tongue range over every subject or warp the truth was said to talk in circles in a manner no different from that of a mongrel who, not knowing the source of alarm, barks in circles (w'geewi-animoh). Ever since words and sounds were reduced to written symbols and have been stripped of their mystery and magic, the regard and reverence for them have diminished.

As rich and full of meaning as may be individual words and expressions, they embody only a small portion of the entire stock and potential of tribal knowledge, wisdom, and intellectual attainment; the greater part is deposited in myths, legends, stories, and in the lyrics of chants that make up the tribe's literature. Therein will be found the essence and the substance of the nation's ideas, attitudes, beliefs, values, and accounts of their institutions and rituals. Without language, scholars, writers and teachers will have no access to the depth and width of Anishinaubae knowledge and understanding, but must continue to belabour, as they have done these many years, under the impression the "Indian" stories are nothing more than Fairy Tales or Folklore, fit only for juvenile minds. For scholars and academics Nana'b'oozoo, Raven, Glooscap, Weesaukeechauk and other mythological figures will ever remain "tricksters"... culture heroes ... deities whose misadventures were dreamed into being only for the amusement of children. Primitive and pagan, and illiterate to boot, "Indians" could not possible address or articulate abstract ideas or themes; neither their minds nor their languages could possibly express any idea more complex than taboos, superstitions and bodily needs.

But were ethnologists, anthropologists, linguists, ... teachers of Native children and writers of Native literature, ... yes, even archaeologists ..., were all these men and women to learn a Native language, perhaps they might learn that Nana'b'oozoo and Raven are not simply "tricksters" but the caricatured representations of human nature and character in their many facets; perhaps they might give thought to the meaning and sense to be found in "Weesaukeechauk," The Bitter Soul. There is no other way except through language for scholars to learn or to validate their studies, their theories, their theses about the values, ideals, institutions or any other aspect of tribal life; there is no other way by which knowledge of Native life can find increase. It is not enough to say in hushed tones after a reverential description of a totem pole or the lacing of a snowshoe, "My, weren't they clever."

Just consider the fate of "Indian" stories written by those who knew nothing of the language, and never did hear any of the stories in their entirety or in their original version, but derived everything that they knew of their subject from second, third and even fourth diluted sources. Is it any wonder, then, that the stories in *Indian Legends of Canada* by E.E. Clark, or in *Manabozho* by T.B. Leekley are so bland and devoid of sense? Had the authors known the stories in their "Indian" sense and flavour, perhaps they might have infused their versions with more wit and substance. Had the authors known that the creation story was intended to represent in the most dramatic way possible the process of individual development from the smallest moiety of talent to be retrieved from the depths of one's being and then given growth by breath of life, they might have written their accounts differently. Thus men and women are to develop themselves from the talent given them, create their own words, shape their being and give meaning to life. Had the authors known this meaning of the Creation Story perhaps they might have written their accounts in terms more in keeping with the sense and thrust of the story. But not knowing the language, nor having heard the story in its original text or state, the authors could not, despite their intentions, impart to their accounts the due weight and perspective the stories deserved. The stories were demeaned.

THINK INDIAN

With language dead and literature demeaned, "Indian" institutions are beyond understanding and restoration. Let us turn back the calendar two-and-a-half centuries, to that period when the "Indian" languages were spoken in every home, when Native literature inspired thought, and when Native "Indian" institutions governed Native "Indian" life. It was then that a Native institution caught the imagination of the newcomers to this continent. The men and women who founded a new nation, to be known as the United States of America, took as their model for their constitution and government the principles of government and administration embodied in The Great Tree of Peace of the Five Nations Confederacy. The institution of The Great Tree of Peace was not then too primitive nor too alien for study or emulation to the founders of the United States. In more recent years even the architects of the United Nations regarded the "Indian" institutions that may well serve and benefit this society and this nation, not as dramatically as did The Great Tree of Peace the United States of America, but to bestow some good as yet undreamed or unimagined. Just how much good such institutions may confer upon this or some future generation will not be known unless the "Indian" languages survive.

And what is it that has undermined the vitality of some of the "Indian" languages and deprived this generation and this society the promise and the benefit of the wisdom and the knowledge embodied in tribal literature?

In the case of the Beothuk and their language, the means used were simple and direct; it was the blade, the bludgeon and the bullet that were plied in the destruction of the Beothuk in their sleep, at their tables, and in their quiet passage from home to place of work, until the tribe was no more. The speakers were annihilated; no more was the Beothuk language spoken; whatever their wisdom or whatever their institutions, the whole of the Beothuk heritage was destroyed.

In other instances, instead of bullets, bludgeons and bayonets, other means were used to put an end to the speaking of an "Indian" language. A kick with a police riding boot administered by a 175 pound man upon the person of an eight year old boy for uttering the language of "a savage" left its pain for days and its bruise upon the spirit for life. A boy once kicked was not likely to risk a second or third. A slap in the face or a punch to the back of the head delivered even by a small man upon the person of a small boy left its sting and a humiliation not soon forgotten. And if a boot or a fist were not administered, then a lash or a yardstick was plied until the "Indian" language was beaten out. To boot and fist and lash was added ridicule. Both speaker and his language were assailed. "What's the use of that language? It isn't polite to speak another language in the presence of other people. Learn English! That's the only way you're going to get ahead. How can you learn two languages at the same time? No wonder kids can't learn anything else. It's a primitive language; hasn't the vocabulary to express abstract ideas. Say 'ugh'. Say something in your language!… How can you get your tongue around those sounds?" On and on the comments were made, disparaging, until in too many the language was shamed into silence and disuse.

And how may the federal government assist in the restoration of the Native languages to their former vigour and vitality, and enable them to fulfill their promise?

The government of Canada must finance the establishment of either provincial or regional language institutions to be affiliated with a university or a provincial Native educational organization. The function of the "institute," to be headed by a Native person who speaks, reads, and writes a Native language, will be to foster research into language and to encourage the publication of lexicons, dictionaries, courses, myths, genealogies, histories, religion, ceremonies, chants, prayers and general articles, to tape these and to build a collection of written and oral literature, and to make the same accessible to scholars, teachers and Native institutions; and to duplicate and distribute written and oral literature to the Native communities and learning institutions. The Native languages deserve to be enshrined in this country's heritage as much as do snowshoes, shards, and arrowheads. Nay! More.

But unless these writings are published and distributed, they can never nurture growth in language or literature. Taking into account the market represented by each tribe, no commercial publisher would risk publication of an "Indian" book. Hence, only the federal government has the means to sponsor publication of an "Indian text," either through a commercial publisher or through The Queen's Printer. The publication of an "Indian" book may not be a commercially profitable enterprise, but it would add to the nation's intellectual and literary heritage.

THE LAND WE CANNOT GIVE

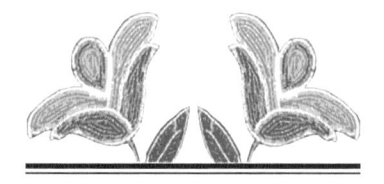

BASIL H. JOHNSTON, O.ONT., LLD., B.A. © 1991

ORIGINALLY PUBLISHED BY GINGER PRESS, OWEN SOUND ONTARIO

THINK INDIAN

The Land We Cannot Give

Dear Neighbour,

I'm sorry to hear that you and many others are disturbed by the growing influx of people from the urban centres to the south into Grey and Bruce counties, and that you are uneasy about the proliferation of "For Sale" signs and the likelihood of severances of land. That you are perturbed by the effects all of this will have on the tone and way of life that you have been accustomed to, I think I can well understand. I am equally certain that our ancestors at Cape Croker and Saugeen, former owners of the entire peninsula, would have understood your agitation. They underwent similar distress about the flood of strangers into these parts a hundred and fifty years ago. In fact, according to a letter written by our tribal ancestors in Owen Sound, dated 1848, they were prepared to take up whatever weapons they could lay their hands on to defend their lands.

There is little doubt that the reasons for your fears are no different from those that troubled our forebears, and your fears are no less groundless.

Your mode of life will be altered just as surely as ours was modified, much as you may hope against its coming to pass, and hard as you may resist it. Our way of life in Saugeen and Cape Croker will too undergo further change.

What can be done to stem the influx or to prevent severance and the eventual inevitable mutation of the way of life? How can the people in the southern Georgian Bay area, Cape Croker, and Saugeen join in common cause?

From your anxiety it is evident that you have formed an attachment for the land, not for the price it may bring but for the way of life it represents. But it is your kindred, the newcomers to the area, who have not the same regard for land that you and all of us share.

The newcomers think of land as "real estate," an "investment," a thing to be bought and sold, a piece of property to be rezoned, severed and developed so that it yields maximum profits. Nor do your urban kin have any more care or respect for the way of life that rural people normally associated with land.

Last year one of Toronto's daily papers published an article on the growing resentment of your neighbours in Wasaga and environs toward the invasion of holiday and vacation visitors, particularly the weekend species. According to that article, most of the people in Wasaga and the adjacent communities objected to more than the blockage of their driveways, the playing of radios and stereos at excessive volumes, and the holding of picnics directly in front of the homes of the residents. It was the litter abandoned by the visitors: bottles, tin cans, bags, plastic and foam plates and cups, and diverse rubbish that really upset residents of Wasaga. Some of the residents then went further, adverting to the interference in their rights and the change in the character of the area, of the impairment inflicted on the beauty, cleanliness and tranquility of the area. When told of the remarks of the residents of Wasaga, a weekender retorted, "What did they expect? Things to remain as they are forever?"

There was not in that comment a hint of regret for the disturbance caused, or for the blight of garbage left behind. There was not a trace of respect for old values. On the contrary, there was a tone of disdain not only for the rights and sensibilities of the residents, but also for the land and the way of life. They have no more respect or reverence for the land than do power and pulp and timber companies or developers who ravage the land for profit.

To such, what argument can be offered that would persuade them that land is more than a mere commodity? What can be said to make them see that land provides us with more than food, clothing, and shelter; that it inspired the country's painters, poets, writers, musicians and playwrights to attempt works of art? It sustains humankind's corporeal as well as its spiritual and intellectual needs.

Our North American Indian ancestors realized this a long time ago when their lives were much more closely bound to the land. When they spoke of land, they referred not only to the soil at their feet, or to a concession. They meant a territory, with its valleys and heights, forests and meadows, lakes and rivers, marshes and outcrops, islands and skies; they had in mind the creatures who share tenure with humankind, the bear and deer, hawks and eagles, snakes and turtles, bees and mosquitoes, pine and clover; they thought of winds and storms, rains and snows, warmth and cold; everything within, above, below. Mother Earth they called her out of respect, reverence, and gratitude for her provision of everything for humankind's material and spiritual needs.

Somehow those old, unschooled people knew that land, and all the things and beings on it, were inseparable, and therefore beyond price. Few have stated this understanding of land better than Crowfoot, a Blackfoot chief. The following account is taken from The Canadian Indian, by Fraser Symington:

In the negotiations preceding the treaty with the Blackfoot Confederacy, Canadian government spokesmen tried to persuade Chief Crowfoot that his people should do as the tribes to the east had done — cede their territories to the Queen and settle down on a reservation. To illustrate the annual "treaty money" payments which would accrue to the Indians, one of the white men spread a number of dollar bills on the ground. This version of the proceedings is taken from Professor E.A. Corbett's book, Blackfoot Trails.

"This is what the White man trades with, this is his buffalo robe. Just as you trade with skins, we trade with these pieces of paper." When the White chief had laid all his money on the ground and shown how much he would give if the Indians would sign a treaty, the red man took a handful of clay and made a ball of it, and put it on the fire and cooked it; it did not crack. Then he said to the White man, "Now put your money on the fire and see if it will last as long as the clay." Then the White chief said, "No, my money will burn because it is made of paper." Then, with an amused gleam in his piercing grey eyes, the old chief said, "Oho, your money is not as good as our land, is it? The wind will blow it away, fire will burn it, water will rot it. Nothing can destroy our land. You don't make a very good trade."

The chief of the Blackfoot picked up a handful of sand from the bank of the Milk River; this he handed to the White man and said, "You count the grains of sand in that while I count the money you offer for my land." The White chief poured the sand into the palm of his hand and said, "I would not live long enough to count this, but you can count that money in a few minutes."

"Very well," said the wise Crowfoot. "Our land is more valuable than your money. It will last forever. It will not perish as long as the sun shines and the water flows, and through all the years it will give life to men and beasts. We cannot sell the lives of men and animals, and therefore we cannot sell the land. It was put here by the Great Spirit, and we cannot sell it because it does not really belong to us. You can count your money and burn it with the nod of a buffalo's head, but only the Great Spirit can count the grains of sand and the blades of grass on these plains. As a present to you we will give you anything we have that you can take with you; the land we cannot give."

And yet, in spite of Crowfoot's resistance and eloquence, his land was sold, and his people's lives changed.

To forestall what you fear there must be a drastic revision in the attitude toward land on the part of your kin. And though it would be gratifying to have people espouse a reverence and an esteem for the land in the same degree as did our North American Indian forebears, it would be presumptuous and quite unnecessary. But it would be well to look at the land not in old terms, but in fresh, as Dr. David Suzuki urges; that humankind's well-being depends upon the health of the earth. When he speaks of the earth—the globe—he includes everything and everyone upon it, not just the soil at his feet.

It is doubtful that this can be done in time to prevent this anticipated influx and the resultant changes that will inevitably follow.

No, neighbour, your life and mine will not be what they used to be, what we had dreamed them to be. We cannot be sure that the water we drink is safe; we cannot be sure that the fish we eat is good for us; we cannot be certain that the air we breathe is unpolluted; we can no longer be as confident as we once were that the waters of Georgian Bay or Lake Huron are safe to swim in.

We can no longer retire to some solitary glade to give in to serenity and peace, there to be uninterrupted by machines. This is now our legacy.

And it is sad. I am sad. But I am sadder for my grandchildren and all the other children.

They deserve an uncontaminated bequest, just as we inherited. Perhaps if you and your kin and all of us had taken up the North American Indian belief that land belongs not to this generation alone, but those still unborn, our grandchildren would look forward to an uncontaminated bequest. They will never know what you and I and our generation took for granted. It is gone.

THINK INDIAN

PREFACE TO

DANCING WITH A GHOST

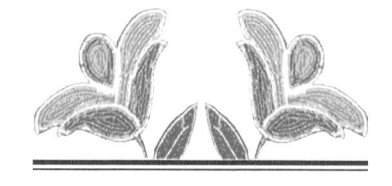

BASIL H. JOHNSTON, O.ONT., LLD., B.A. © 1991

Preface To

Dancing With A Ghost

For years the missionaries had been pressing the Six Nations peoples and other North American Indians to forsake their manitous and uncivilized ways and to espouse the Bible and civilization. Finally, in 1805, the Six Nations peoples granted a missionary an interview. On behalf of the people Red Jacket, a celebrated Seneca orator, rejected the missionaries' overture with the words in his language that meant "Kitchi-Manitou has given us a different understanding."

Although he was speaking on behalf of the Six Nations peoples, Red Jacket's remarks applied with equal force to other North American cultures. To the Six Nations peoples and their neighbours, it was quite clear even then that the notions, ideas, values, perceptions, ideals, beliefs, institutions, insights, opinions, aspirations, concepts, customs, habits, practices, conventions, outlooks that they embraced were different from those held by the newcomers.

In rejecting the invitation to conversion, and preferring to cling to and abide by their traditional understandings, Red Jacket did not say or imply that he was doing so because his peoples' understandings were better and that of the newcomer worse. Rather, the missionaries had not shown their beliefs and conduct to be superior to the knowledge and learning that Kitchi-Manitou had bestowed upon and had served them well. And by crediting Kitchi-Manitou as the Benefactor of these understandings, Red Jacket was saying in just another way that his peoples' understandings possessed the same weight as those of others.

When Red Jacket uttered that one sentence, "Kitchi-Manitou has given us a different understanding," he was referring to all the differences, great and small, palpable and impalpable, adverse and akin that separated the Brown People and the White. Moreover, Red Jacket used the pronoun "us" to convey the notion that his people collectively espoused these understandings, conceptions because they coincided with their own individual thoughts and ideas, and sustained the nations. Yet even though men and women shared common beliefs and heritage, they also upheld the individual's rights to declare "Kitchi-Manitou has given me a different understanding."

As such, common and individual understandings originating with Kitchi-Manitou gave them a sacrosanct aspect. The mode by which men and women gain these understandings, through dream and vision, is also almost sacrosanct. Having their origin with Kitchi-Manitou and coming to individuals through the milieu of the world of the manitous, these understandings merited respect and deference.

In purpose, different understandings, notions, ideas, points of view, perceptions were meant, it was supposed, to illuminate, enlighten and to enhance individual as well as general knowledge. Men and women were expected to weigh, not reject outright, opinions different from their own, and to clarify their own ideas and enrich their general understandings. At the same time it was expected that men and women so doing would find merit in the ideas of others, and accord those others due credit for the worth of their ideas.

To abandon one's opinion of belief, or even to alter one's conviction or position, has seldom been easy. To do so is regarded as akin to an admission that one's opinions were not as good as those of another.

It is equally difficult for men and women who still speak their ancestral languages to disown all or any portion of their cultural heritage that they know is as substantive as any other, and one that still has meaning and application and purpose.

And what bearing does the adherence to traditional views and customs by North American Indians have upon their relationships with this country's governments, agencies and institutions? How does the adherence to traditional views and custom bear upon the provision of government services and programs? How does adherence to traditional values bear upon national and provincial dreams, aspirations and plans? How does adherence to traditional values affect North American Indians' entry into and participation in this country's business and academic affairs?

Of course, questions of like character, stripe and tone can be put to Canadians of European ancestry. How is the general unwillingness of White Society to acknowledge and recognize that North American Indians have different understandings and values and institutions that have not lost their relevance and application despite 500 years of cultural and technological advances influence their affairs with the original peoples?

It is this: as long as the governments and the officials of this country, through its agencies and institutions, fail to acknowledge and recognize that many original peoples of this country have different values and institutions and still cling to them; and so long as they believe and insist that the original peoples abandon their ancestral heritage and embrace European culture, so long will penalties be unconscionably imposed upon the Natives, and injustices, wrongs and injuries be committed. And so long as the government and the officials of this country continue to act as if the original peoples are the only ones in need of instruction and improvement, so long will suspicion and distrust persist.

But if Canadians of European heritage were willing to grant, just as their ancestors had done so two, three, four and five hundred years ago, that North American Indian values and institutions are not only different but substantive as well, with the potential to add to the well-being and good will of this country, then not only would Canadians of European ancestry benefit, indeed everyone would gain.

Now there are many differences between the original peoples and Canadians of overseas origin on a wide range of matters from attitudes, insights, aspirations, religion, customs, institutions, values, beliefs, outlooks to ideals; nay, in almost every aspect of human life; some poles apart, some not so distant. Within the limits of this preface only a brief sketch is possible. I will dwell briefly on three or perhaps four differences that bear upon my fellow Natives in their experiences with the administration of justice in this country.

From the moment that European missionaries set eyes on North American Indians they assumed that the Brown-skinned Natives were pagan and quite incapable of grasping or expressing abstract ideas such as "God," or postulating divine attributes. The missionaries believed that at best the aboriginal mind could posit the existence of little spirits and conduct superstitious rituals and ceremonies. What the North American Indians needed was the Bible and education to draw them from the path of error and set them on the path of truth.

But the aborigines already had a word, "manitou," in the vocabulary to express the different states and forms of incorporeal being and existence. They said "manitouwun" to refer to the healing properties of a plant; "manitouwut" to refer to the mystical attributes of a setting; "w'manitouwih" to refer to the prophetic gift of seers. Kitchi-Manitou was God, the Great and Foremost Mystery of the Supernatural and natural orders. With these terms and their usage the aborigines gave evidence of their recognition and sense that there was something more to being and existence than physical, concrete reality.

Because Kitchi-Manitou was a being existing in the supernatural sphere and order, Kitchi-Manitou was beyond human experience, knowledge and description. But it was taken for granted and accepted as true that Kitchi-Manitou created the universe, the world and the beings upon, above and below, both corporeal and incorporeal, from a vision or dream. Creation, by which the mystical vision was brought into the being of physical reality, was seen as an act of generosity and a sharing of one's goods with those in need.

The men and women who were created as the last and most dependent of all beings took the Native in its collective form "Anishinaubaek" for themselves. Such a designation represented their understanding of the fundamental goodness of human nature derived from the supposition that men and women generally meant well in all their undertakings and aspirations. The name also represented the good opinion they had of themselves as men and women of merit. This conviction and belief in the essential goodness of purpose and intent of human beings remained steadfast despite human experience and the evidence of history that showed that men and women seemed more often than not to have failed to fulfill their good intentions and committed considerable harm in the process. The belief in the innate goodness of human nature remained, and conferred on men and women a sense of worth, equality, and pride.

There was another source for this sense of worth and purpose. In each person there was implanted by Kitchi-Manitou a seed or a small clutch of talent within his innermost being. This was the substance that each person was to seek through dream and vision and having taken possession of it, create his being, his world and his sphere with it in emulation of Kitchi-Manitou.

But to quest for a vision and then having received it, bring it to fulfillment, has never been an easy undertaking. Human frailties such as fear and sloth, selfishness and impulsiveness, jealousy and inconstancy, conceit and irreverence, lust and temper may daunt, dupe and withhold men and women in their quest and in their efforts to fulfill their visions. Such men and women who have been discouraged or misled in their quest, or prevented from carrying out their visions or from discharging their duties and in the course caused pain and injury were regarded as having stumbled or lost their way or been led astray by malevolent manitous. What those who stumbled or lost their way or, by failing to do what they ought have done, wronged one of their kin or neighbours, needed, was to be given a helping hand, redirected and counselled. Besides guidance, those who had done serious harm were expected to purify themselves in a sweat lodge and to petition the manitous for good dreams.

Apart from their presumed worth, their practical lives had as much to do with men's and women's self-esteem. In days gone by men and women hunted, trapped, fished, harvested and prepared medicines to feed, clothe, shelter and to keep themselves in good health. There was then ample opportunity for everyone to render some good service to family and community. The training, the equipment, the experience, the opportunities and the needs were similar. In such circumstances no man or woman was inferior to any other. And if further proof was needed to show or to establish the essential equality of men and women, isolation was pointed out as the one sphere in which men and women could show that they were as good, no worse than any other. To face and surmount similar challenges and tests alone, without aid, was the measure by which men and women judged others and loved to be judged. It was from service to family and community that men and women derived their sense of worth and pride. Every person was worth something, not only to himself but to the entire community.

THINK INDIAN

To set aside enough food to last them through the winter was what drove men and women to labour the summer through till the first fall of snow. If they failed to store enough food, they and their families faced hardship and the prospect of eating bark, frozen berries and moss. But if their labours had been rewarded, they could all look forward to the forthcoming winter with confidence and security.

Then they could listen to tribal historians recount tribal accomplishments; they could listen to tribal raconteurs describe and explain the origin and nature of things and the meanings of customs, rituals and ceremonies; and they could listen to accounts of Nanabush, the central figure in Anishinaubae literature, representing what they understood of human nature.

The Anishinaubaek had a high regard akin to reverence for storytellers, orators, and for language itself. The highest compliment or tribute they could pay a speaker was to say of him or her "w'daeb-awae," taken to mean "he/she is right, correct, accurate, truthful." It is an expression approximating the word for "truth" in the English language except that it means that one casts one's knowledge as far as one has perceived it and as accurately as one can describe it given one's command of language. In other words, the best one can do is to tell what one knows with the highest degree of accuracy. Beyond this one cannot go. According to this understanding there is or can be no such thing as absolute truth.

For the Anishinaubae peoples to say "w'daeb-awae" of another person was payment of a compliment, and in so doing they were affirming that person's credibility at the same time. They were associating and binding speech and credibility. It was a delicate relationship that could easily be broken by the careless use of speech. Once the bond was broken, trust and confidence in the speaker was lost. The speaker no longer had an influence with an audience. For a community of persons or society to regard a person as one worth listening to was the highest distinction they could confer upon another.
By the same token, the worst epithet that the Anishinaubae peoples could impose on any would-be speaker was to say "w'geewi-animoh," meaning that he or she talks in circles as a dog barks in all directions in uncertainty as to the source of some unknown disturbance.

There are different understandings of human nature and conduct and speech as they bear upon the human experience, and relationships ought not to divide or alienate. But the sad fact is that they do. In almost every sphere, be it street, school, church, marketplace where men and women of North American heritage meet Canadians of West European heritage there occurs what sociologists call a cultural conflict from which North American Indians are forced to give ground, suffer losses and pay a price by virtue of the odds mounted against them.

Frequent as are these clashes, none are more dramatic or as traumatic or as enduring as those that take place within the jurisdiction of the law and within the courts of justice.

If a man or woman had the misfortune of breaking one of the country's laws, he or she, depending upon the gravity of the charge, would be clapped into jail soon after arrest. On a lesser charge an accused may be allowed his freedom on bail. For serious offences the accused, from the moment of charge and arrest, is regarded as a felon, a criminal, a being of little worth, quite unfit to be free in the society of law abiding citizens. That person belongs in jail with other men and women of his ilk, with the guilty and the wicked, in exile, ostracized.

But it is in the courtroom where the accused is made to appear as a base person. The Crown introduces evidence to support its charges and to obtain a verdict of guilty, and demands the imposition of the maximum penalty, removal from the society of good men and women, and sentence to the company of bad men and bad women. Counsel assails the accused's self-esteem, pride, sense of worth and credibility. The accused's counsel may rebut the charges and obtain an acquittal, but if defence counsel is unsuccessful and his client is found and pronounced guilty as charged, the accused's wickedness is confirmed and upheld by the court, and reported in the papers.

In the proceedings and in the court the accused, now a prisoner, is insignificant. The court belongs to the judge and the lawyers, especially the lawyers. They are the contestants, the principal actors who command the attention of the spectators, as Perry Mason overshadowed everyone else in the television court with his cleverness, wit, knowledge of the law and eloquence. In their arguments they are, it seems, preoccupied with the accused's offence, which may have been his first and only offence, a preoccupation that magnifies the offence while burying the basic decency and good of the person in the dock. The accused doesn't amount to much.

Even in the hierarchy of the court the accused is consigned to the lowest place in the scale. Next in rank above him are his captors, the police officers. Still higher in standing, importance and in education are the lawyers. At the top and presiding over all else is the judge. The accused is a prisoner, opposed by the Crown. He or she is of little consequence, to be commanded to rise and to sit down, to speak and to be silent.

To be confined in a stall, perhaps even manacled and commanded as a slave is ordered about, is as demeaning as a human being can be made to endure. It compares to what victorious warriors once did to captives, to bind them and, if possible, force them to perform menial labours as beasts of burden, "wukaunuk," and cast them scraps to eat. Rather than yield, many men and women defied their captors and chose torture and death.

And just as the accused is forced to put his self esteem and dignity on the line, so must he his credibility. He is made to swear to "tell the truth, the whole truth, and nothing but the truth, so help you God!" And so he does, to the best of his recollection, according as he perceived it and as well as his command of language will enable him ... and as much or as little as the lawyers want introduced into the course of the trial as will advance their respective causes. But the answers the accused gives and the evidence witnesses provide are not good enough for the Crown or the accused's counsel. The lawyers are not satisfied with discrediting testimony but it seems they are intent upon destroying whoever is summoned to the dock. That they should destroy liars and perjurers is fitting. But for lawyers with the ability to make anyone appear like a liar and a fool to set about to assault and destroy credibility is an abuse of skill and authority.

The accused and the witnesses are forced to run the judicial gauntlet and are made to suffer dishonour, disgrace and even vilification at the hands of the lawyers.

What then is to be done? How avoid the ordeal? How is one to survive the ordeal in court and emerge with at least a measure of self-esteem and pride and credibility salvaged? If the accused is innocent, will he end up in prison, as did Donald Marshall or Milton Born With a Tooth, or deported and turned over to the American authorities as was Leonard Pelletier, also in prison? Plead "Guilty" to be done with it quickly and with the least amount of pain seems to be the prevailing attitude.

But suppose the accused is convicted. What hope is there for him in prison? Cast among hardened criminals, men and women deemed incorrigible, some of whom undoubtedly are, what are his prospects? In such milieu, incarcerated with men and women regarded as misfits and who may even regard themselves as unfit, how is a person to maintain his sense of worth and pride; how is such a one to keep from losing his self esteem and begin believing that he is without purpose or of service to himself, to his family and to his community; how is such a man or woman, cut off from his kin and friends, to receive inspiration and encouragement and declaration of faith in his fundamental decency and good will? And segregated from those who know him, how is a man or woman to be set on his feet if he has stumbled, or re-directed to his way if he has gone astray?

Since the mid-sixties many lawyers and judges have taken up the cause for the First Nations peoples, appealing for justice in the courts and for liberality and good will in the social and economic pales. Together, the First Nations peoples and their advocates have blazed a trail some distance. There is still some distance to attain justice for all.

If Mr. Rupert Ross can convince his learned friends to look anew at the adversarial character of litigation and to examine the First Nations peoples' concept of human nature and human misconduct and their matter of setting right an errant man or woman, he will have performed a service of great benefit in recognizing and affirming the substantiveness of these other understandings. And if by some wild chance, at some point beyond the present vision, the justice system of this country were to espouse and adopt the First Nations peoples' concepts and subjoin them to their own, then the administration of justice would gain a greater measure of equity and fairness than it previously had.

THINK INDIAN

THE MODERN WEENDIGOES

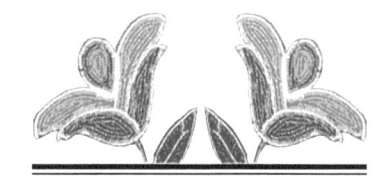

BASIL H. JOHNSTON, O.ONT., LLD., B.A. © 1991

The Modern Weendigoes

Once woods and forests mantled most of this land, this continent. It was the home of the Anishinaubaek (Ojibway, Ottawa, Pottawatomi, Algonquin [sic]), their kin and their neighbours; it was also the home of the moose, the deer, the caribou, the bear, their kindred and their neighbours; it was, as well, the home of the thrushes, the sparrows, the hawks, the tanagers, the ravens, the owls, their cousins and their neighbours; mosquitoes, butterflies, caterpillars, ants, moths, their kind and their neighbours had a place therein. Not only was it home, but it was a wellspring from which all drew their sustenance, medicine, and their knowledge.

Also dwelling in the woods and forests were Weendigoes, giant cannibals who fed upon human flesh, and only human flesh, to allay their perpetual hunger. They stalked villages and camps, waiting for, and only for, the improvident, the slothful, the gluttonous, the promiscuous, the injudicious, the insatiable, the selfish, the avaricious, the wasteful, to be foolish enough to venture alone beyond the environs of their homes in winter. But no matter how many victims a single Weendigo may have devoured raw, he could never requite his hunger. Instead, the more he ate, the larger he grew, and the larger he grew, the greater his hunger. The Weendigo's hunger always remained in proportion to his size.

Even though a Weendigo is a mythical figure, he does represent a real human cupidity. What the old storytellers meant to project in the image of the Weendigo was a universal and unchanging human disposition. But more learned people declared that no such monster ever existed, and that he was a product of superstitious minds and imaginations.

As a result, the Weendigo was driven from his place in Anishinaubae traditions and culture, and ostracized by disbelief and skepticism. It was assumed, and indeed it appeared as if the Weendigo and his brothers and sisters had passed into the Great Beyond, like many North American Indian beliefs and practices and traditions.

Actually, the Weendigoes did not die out or disappear; they have only been assimilated and reincarnated as corporations, conglomerates and multi-nationals. They've even taken on new names, acquired polished manners, and have renounced their cravings for raw human flesh for more refined viands. But their cupidity is no less insatiable than that of their ancestors.

One breed subsists entirely on forests. When this one particular breed beheld forests, its collective cupidity was bestirred as it looked upon an endless, boundless sea of green, green, green, green, as in greenbacks. They saw beyond, even into the future. Money. Cash. Deposit. Bank Accounts. Interest. Reserves. Investments, securities, bonds, shares, interest dividends, capital gains, assets, funds, deals, revenue, income, prosperity, opulence, profits, riches, wealth, comfort. Never would they have need.

They recruited woodsmen with axes, cross-cut saws and Swede, sputters, shovels, cant hooks, grapples, chains, ropes, files and pikes, and sent them into woods and forests to fell, hew, saw, cut, chop, slash and level the trees.

The forests resounded with the clash of axes and the whine of saws as blades bit into the flesh of spruce, pine, cedar, tamarack and poplar to fulfill the demands of the Weendigoes in Toronto, Montreal, Vancouver, New York, Chicago, Boston, wherever they now dwelt. Cries of "Timber!" echoed and re-echoed across the treetops, followed by the rip and tear of splintering trees. Then, finally, the crash that thundered throughout the bush.

And as fast as woodsmen felled the trees, teamsters delivered sleighload after sleighload to railway sidings and to rivers. Train after train, shipload after shipload of timber, logs and pulp were delivered to mills.

Yet fast as the woodsmen cut, and much as they hewed down, it was never fast enough; the quantity always fell short of the demands and expectations of the Weendigoes, their masters.

"Is that all? Should there not be more? We demand a bigger return for our risks and our investments. Only more will satisfy us. Any amount will do, so long as it's more, but the more the better."

The demands for more speed and more pulp, more timber, and more logs were met. Axes, saws, woodsmen, sleighs, horses and teamsters were replaced, and their blows and calls no longer rang in the forest. Instead, in their place, chain saws whined, caterpillar tractors with huge blades bulled and battered their way through the forest, uprooting trees to clear the way for automatic shearers that topped, limbed, and sheared the trunks. These mechanical Weendigoes gutted and desolated the forests, leaving death, destruction and ugliness where once there was life, abundance, and beauty.

Trucks and transports, faster and bigger than horses and sleds, operated day and night delivering cargo in size and in speed that their predecessors, horses and sleighs, could never match.

Yet the Weendigoes wanted still more, and it didn't matter if their policies and practices of clear cutting in their harvest of timber and pulp resulted in violations of North American Indian rights or in the further impairment of their lives, just as it didn't matter to them that their modus operandi resulted in the permanent defilement of hillside and mountainside by erosion. They are indifferent to the carnage inflicted upon bears, wolves, rabbits, thrushes, sparrows, warblers. Who cares if they are displaced? What possible harm has been done? Nor does it seem as if these modern Weendigoes have any regard for the rights of future generations to the yield of Mother Earth.

Profit, wealth, comfort, power is the end of business. Anything that detracts from or diminishes the anticipated return, be it taking pains not to violate the rights of others, or taking measures to ensure that the land remains fertile and productive for future generations, must, it seems, be circumvented.

And what has been the result of this self-serving, self-glutting disposition? Why? In ten short decades these modern Weendigoes have accomplished what at one time seemed impossible; they have laid waste immense tracts of forest that were seen as beyond limit as well as self-propagating, ample enough to serve this generation and many more to come. Now, as the forests are in decline, the Weendigoes are looking at a future that offers scarcity, while many people are assessing the damage done by these Weendigoes, not in terms of dollars but in terms of the damage inflicted upon the environment and the climate, and on botanical and zoological life.

The new, reincarnated Weendigoes are no different from their forebears. They are even more omnivorous than their old ancestors. The only difference is that the modern, reincarnated Weendigoes wear elegant clothes and comport themselves with an air of cultured and dignified respectability.

THINK INDIAN

"IRON RAY"

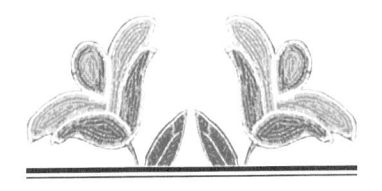

BASIL H. JOHNSTON, O.ONT., LLD., B.A. © 1992

"Iron Ray"

I wish to dedicate this tribute to one soldier in particular, Corporal Ray Nadjiwon, deceased, but in so doing I mean to pay tribute to all soldiers of North American Indian ancestry who served in Canada's armed forces in World War One, World War Two, in the Korean War, as well as in the Vietnam War, in the cause of peace, freedom, rights and justice not only for Canada's citizens but for their own peoples. It can only be hoped that they have not served in vain.

While we were at school, stalled in the primary grades, Ray (Nadjiwon) was our leader, a person we looked up to. First of all he was not much older than we were, only a grade or two ahead of the rest of us, maybe even three, but he was much bigger than we were, bigger than most of the boys in grade eight, as big as a man. He was already rugged, muscular, raw-boned, ruddy-faced, hair rumpled, a Huckleberry Finn type. By his physique and disposition he was meant not for books or classrooms, but for the outdoors, hard labour, and daring.

In school our idol earned more reproofs and strappings than he did awards or honours. But no matter how many stripes Miss Burke delivered upon his hands, she could not make Ray cry, wince, or flinch. It seemed as if he was immune to pain. After punishment no one can remember Ray expressing anything resembling resentment toward the teacher.

Playing outside after school Ray was our leader in games both innocent and mischievous. In a way he was our guardian and foil, for nothing could hurt him; he was immune and as long as we were in his presence no harm could come to us. Besides, if we failed to get home on time, we could always blame Ray.

We watched him break a thin sheet of ice covering the gravel pit pool behind the Nadjiwon homestead, then enter the frigid waters and afterward emerge without shivering. With a laugh he dared us to follow his example. He invited us to strike his chest and stomach as hard as we could with our fists. But none of our blows made the slightest impression upon him. Our admiration grew. In winter he seldom wore mittens or a hat. Unlike others who suffered frostbite and pneumonia for neglecting to wear these garments, Ray sustained not even a headache. A wagon wheel ... or was it a sleigh runner ... or was it both at different times, passed over his legs. Ray sustained only a bruise. And he could eat uncooked meat, and even inedible parts without enduring indigestion. Nothing could hurt Ray. He was indestructible, like iron. Yes, like iron. Someone called him Iron Ray, and the name stuck.

In 1939 World War Two broke out. All the able bodied men and several young women, some as young as fifteen, enlisted within a few days of Canada's declaration of war. As soon as he was sixteen, Iron Ray also volunteered, taking his place by the side of his older brothers, kin, neighbours, and friends who flocked to the colours in such numbers that Cape Croker earned the distinction of being the community with the highest average of its able bodied men and women serving in the armed forces of any community in Canada.

Of this contingent too many never came back home. Many more were wounded. All Ray suffered was a flesh wound. Nothing else touched him; not bombs, shells, tracers, shrapnel, bayonets, or mines. He was at the front in Italy and, from the day the invasion of Europe was launched by the Allied Forces until German capitulated on V.E. Day, Ray offered his life, but the enemy could not take it. He was as indestructible in war as he was in peacetime.

He was as fine a soldier as any, but he won no honours, no medals for valour, no mention in dispatches or citations, not even a ribbon for good conduct. But he was just as proud of his many campaign and battle ribbons as the men who had been awarded medals for courage beyond the call of duty. For his indestructibility Ray was promoted to the rank of corporal. Those who served under him declared they would follow him anywhere.

When World War Two was over, Ray remained in the army, intending to make it a career because he was not prepared or trained for any other. He fell in love and married Clarty (Clara) Keeshig, who had also served overseas. Ray became husband and father.

War broke out once more, this time in Korea. Among the many men from Cape Croker serving in Korea was Iron Ray. He did so not out of love for war but for a cause, a cause that he could not well articulate when asked, except to say that "it's so's people can live in peace."

Again Ray served in the front lines without incurring wound or hurt, then returned to civilian life.

For young men like Ray, without adequate education, training or skills, what were the prospects at home, elsewhere? What goal, career, dream, reward could they aspire to? What could they look forward to in the future? Not much. Not much more than manual labour in lumber camps, mines, and in construction.

Luckily, in those days there was ample opportunity in those industries, and Iron Ray found work as an iron-worker on high steel, an occupation meant only for those with nerves of iron, ice in their veins and certainty in their footing. No occupation could have better suited Iron Ray. It was meant for him and he for it, and it sustained him and his family until company regulations governing age forced him to retire. But during the time that he worked in an industry known for its high risks and the proportionately high rate of accidents, Ray sustained nary a scratch.

He came home to the village where he grew up, where age at last began to overtake him, whitening his hair and slowing his step. But he was still indifferent to his personal well-being, as careless as he had been fifty years before. Perhaps he didn't feel the cold or the discomfort wrought by rain, sleet, hail and wind. Perhaps he had a much higher tolerance for discomfort than most people. But nothing seemed to bother him, nothing.

Though he was retired and pensioned, the pension was not sufficient to exempt him from work. Ray still had to seek employment; fishing, cutting wood, and pruning trees. Besides, he was more accustomed to labour than he was to leisure.

In the early morning of June 13, 1988, as Ray slept on the couch in the front room, fire broke out in the home where he was staying. By the time that he awakened to the cries of Baby Courtnie, the flames had razed the roof and were clawing their way downwards, black acrid choking smoke glutted the interior, and poured out shattered windows and the ravaged roof.

A neighbour saw the fire and gave alarm at once. Within minutes the Fire Brigade was at the scene. They brought the blaze under control, then put it out.

When the members of the Fire Department deemed it safe to enter the derelict, they found Iron Ray wedged behind the door and under some collapsed rafters. In his arms, cradled close to his chest, he held the baby. Ray was dead; the baby was dead.

Iron Ray finally paid the supreme sacrifice. But before he died, he had led Violet (Elliot) and a boy, Peter, to safety. He returned into the inferno for the baby. He had fought his way through smoke and flame to the baby's room and crib, and fought and groped his way out as far as the door. He got no further. Fire and smoke overtook and overwhelmed him and the baby. Fire had done what neither men and their weapons and the elements had failed to do, hurt and kill him. Ray gave his life not in battle for high causes, but in the safety and security of home, for the sake of a baby.

The inscription on his tombstone is simple. It reads: "Corporal Raymond Nadjiwon. Died June 13, 1988." It should have included "Greater love hath no man than this, that a man lay down his life for his friends."

WALTER "CHICK" JOHNSTON

"HE WAS A GOOD MAN"

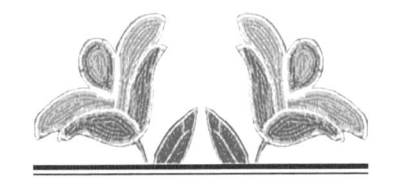

BASIL H. JOHNSTON, O.ONT., LLD., B.A. © 1992

Walter "Chick" Johnston

"He Was A Good Man"

To the Chippewas of Nawash at Cape Croker, Ontario, Walter Johnston was "Chick," Tribal Secretary, councillor, and band employee for over 50 years; to his sons and daughters he was "Pom;" to me he was "Prof." All were terms of endearment, affection and respect for a man who was indeed "filled with the milk of human kindness."

Yet life was not as generous with Prof as it might have been, as he deserved.

Until his father's death, Prof's mother, Rosa, and his brothers Rufus, Robert and John, had never known need. Life was good; the morrow and the years to come boded well.

But the good life and the promises came to an end when Prof was only three. Edwin, father of Walter, Rufus, Robert and John, died of leukemia at the age of 37. With his father's passing, Prof never knew or experienced the joy and the tenderness of walking with his hand enclosed in that of his father's. Instead, he saw his mother cry and he knew not why.

At three he was too young to know that the good life was no more, and that hardship had begun. Prof and his brothers John and Bobby played as if nothing had happened.

While at play with his brothers, Prof suffered an injury to his foot that was believed to be no worse than a sprain that would heal with rest. But the injury did not mend as expected. Instead it grew into a lump on his instep. From the day that he hurt his foot, "Prof" never again walked normally; he walked as if he had a club-foot, nor could he wear a shoe as other people did. To get his foot into a shoe, it had to be slit to allow his foot to fit in. Yet, according to his brothers, Prof never once complained that his foot pained him, although it must have.

No longer able to run, let alone walk normally, Prof could not take part in the sports that he loved. He could only watch. But if he could not play the games that other boys played, he was not disabled from pursuing the arts, music, reading and writing. He mastered the trumpet, alto, baritone and bass. And from his reading Prof developed a flair for writing. To be able to read, write and count was the utmost that the people of his generation were expected to accomplish, and if more had been expected and demanded, Prof would have measured up to the challenge.

That injury to his foot did more than prevent Prof from running and playing; it prevented him from ever obtaining gainful employment that required physical fitness and strength. While his brothers, kin and neighbours left home to seek work elsewhere, Prof had to stay at home, a cripple, with little to offer to any employer, anywhere.

The outlook was bleak. Yet, despite an unpromising future and despite the antipathy of churches toward mixed marriages, Prof and Frances Nawash married. In marrying, both Prof and auntie were testing the churches and the future.

Prof cut and hewed logs to build his own house. He and Frances did what they could to make ends meet for themselves and their family; growing their own food and harvesting it from meadows and woods. He cut his own wood and earned the occasional dollar or a cut of meat by helping farmers in the high season. Still, he and Frances fell short of providing for their needs. To make up for the shortfall, as did other people, they asked for and received credit from the merchants, did without, and wore used clothing.

Still, Prof was happy.

It was his habit of attending band council meetings that gave Prof a small break. When the Band Council secretary resigned, Prof was asked to take up the duties of recording Band Council business. The stipend for such service was more nominal than adequate such as it was, but it did ease the burden. As secretary, Prof served the community with distinction and diligence and accuracy for years.

Early in his term as Tribal Secretary, Prof made up his mind to write the history of Cape Croker, some day. He did in fact start.

But that work was interrupted when the first of his homes was destroyed by fire. In that fire everything was burned. Of the setback Prof said that

Kitchi-Manitou could not be blamed for the disaster. It was meant to be, and nothing could be done to undo what was meant to be except to start over. With the help of neighbours, Prof and Frances started over.

Not many years later a second home was destroyed by fire, and with it his manuscript. As he looked over the desolation of the charred and smoldering ruins, Prof neither shed a tear or cursed the fates. He thanked Kitchi-Manitou for allowing his family to escape unhurt. He rebuilt his home and rewrote the manuscript.

A third house went up in flames. But not even this latest disaster could unsettle Prof's equanimity or shake his faith in the goodness of God.

At last, many years later, Prof went to Toronto for surgery that would remove the growth from his instep and allow him to walk normally and wear a shoe normally. For the first time since childhood Prof was able to wear a shoe the way it was meant to be worn, but that was all that the operation achieved. Prof was grateful that he could at last wear a shoe and tie the laces.

Of the doctors he said "they did their best." He could no more find fault with them than he could with other men and women.

When asked his opinion of others he would reply, "He is a good man. She is a good woman," and he meant it. Prof was too full of the milk of human kindness to say anything unkind of another, to raise his voice in anger, or to bear malice toward anyone. What he said of others must be said of him, "He was a good man."

In 1976 his beloved wife of 45 years passed away, and half of his being went with her. Prof didn't show his grief, but it was there in the depths of his soul and spirit.

Prof was now alone, the sole survivor of the Edwin Johnston family. He, the cripple, the ill-fated, had outlived his stronger, healthier brothers, kin and friends. At 80 Prof ought to have lived his remaining years as a grandfather and tribal elder, in peace and in security. But the fates were not yet done with this gentle old man. They meant to break him.

THINK INDIAN

One day as he started cooking his meal of eggs, the grease in the pan burst into flame. Burning liquid, lava-hot, flared up and drenched Prof's face, arms, neck, chest.

An ambulance rushed the stricken old man to the Wellesley Street Hospital in Toronto. There he lingered for days at the abyss, held to this side of life only by tubes and his will. The flames and burning grease seared and scarred his body and knotted his hands, but it did not take his life or singe his spirit.

But not even this latest setback daunted "Prof." Months later, as he tried to uncurl his fingers and massage them to movement, Prof spoke of picking up the pieces and rewriting his manuscript when his hands got better. Except that his hands did not heal as Prof hoped they would.

The last time that I saw "Prof" he let me know that his hands were getting better, and flexed his fingers to show me. Sadly, before they became well enough to hold a pencil, Prof fell ill. His family took him to the Wiarton General Hospital.

One of his visitors, Donna Akiwenzie, kin by ancestry, greeted Prof as she was in the habit of greeting him, "Well, president! How do you feel?"

"Well, president! I feel that I will soon meet the most important president of all," Prof said with the same equanimity as he had accepted all the little blessings and hardships that life had bestowed upon him.

And so it was. Prof went to meet the First of Presidents on April 20, 1992, in his 87th year.

If Kitchi-Manitou, the First of Presidents, grants that all men and women be made whole in the next life, and that all suffering come to an end, may the God of all grant that Prof be made whole and live a new existence free of pain and suffering.

Farewell, "Prof," Uncle.

Languages Are Beyond Price

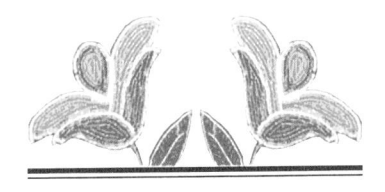

Basil H. Johnston, O.Ont., LLD., B.A. © December 1993

Published in Turtle Quarterly, Niagara Falls, NY, U.S.A., Spring-Summer 1993.

THINK INDIAN

Languages Are Beyond Price

This past winter the Council of the City of Sault Ste. Marie in Ontario, inspired by their mayor, passed a motion decreeing that, owing to the costs involved, no French languages services, medical or otherwise, would be provided to anyone, resident or visitor, regardless of need of circumstances. Like sheep, dozens of other municipalities passed similar motions. Yes, it could cost far too much to provide either a French speaking doctor or nurse or even an interpreter to any man or woman, resident or visitor, who might fall ill in these municipalities of brotherly love. French speaking Canadians, with their passage and application of Bill 101, are not exactly models of tolerance and liberality either. That motions, by-laws and bills restricting the use of French or English, or any other language for that matter, would eventually be passed was inevitable. For years people have disapproved of other languages, expressing their displeasure in various ways. "What's the use of that language? What good does it do? How's it going to help you get ahead? Why speak another language? What gibberish are you speaking? It's not polite to speak another language in company. This is an English speaking country. Why not recognize that English is an international language; that it is the language of the business world? Your language is incapable of expressing abstract ideas. They came here, they should give up their languages if they want to be Canadians." Now at last the many who objected to any language with a foreign tone and accent, and longed for unilingualism to extend from coast to coast, received their wish from the good fairies with the passage of motions, by-laws and bills that restricted languages other than their own.

It was this same temperament that inspired the West Europeans who settled in this country to attempt to drive or starve the North American Indian Native languages into extinction. In the case of the unfortunate Beothuk, the objective was accomplished with rifles; both Beothuk and their language were exterminated. No more Beothuk, no more Beothuk language. The fate of the Beothuk and their language is more than symbolic; it is portentous.

After all these years of relentless pressure and assault, only three of the original 53 North American Indian languages spoken by the North American Indians living in Canada are expected to survive several more generations, Anishinaubae (Ojibway, Ottawa, Pottawatomi, and Algonquin), Cree and Inuktitut; the rest are at the edge of extinction. And while it may be reassuring to learn that Ojibway, Cree and Inuktitut are in relatively sound health, no one should be beguiled by the phrase "several more generations." It is no different from that of a doctor's pronouncement following an examination of a cancer patient that the victim may survive several more months. It is only by understanding the brevity of a "generation" in the life span of a nation, and that life is but a generation from extinction that the Native peoples and Canadians will appreciate the gravity of the malaise that afflicts the Native languages. Soon they will all have passed away.

And what reasons are there, if any, to bemoan their passing?

Has not the renunciation of the Native's ancestral languages and the concomitant espousal of either English or French brought the Micmac, Haida, Blackfoot, and other Native peoples the benefits and advantages of their adopted languages. Did the command of either English or French languages hasten the grant of the franchise? Did it accelerate the bestowal of citizenship? Did it quicken the pace to Bay Street and the corporate boardrooms? Did it clear the way to autonomy in the management of Band and community affairs? Did it secure invitations to membership in the social and service clubs and associations in the nearby municipalities? Did it inspire the good will of the Ministers of Indian Affairs and draw them to the negotiation table? And did the renunciation of Delaware or Seneca or Kamloops procure greater respect and good will? I'm afraid not. What giving up the ancestral languages and adopting the West European languages gained was access to the considerable literary and religious heritage of Western Europe.

But these benefits and advantages could have been earned without sacrificing an ancestral language. Perhaps the promises of success, social acceptance, education, cultural refinement, opportunities implicit in the exhortation "Learn English; Learn French!" were too seductive to resist. As a result, the old neglected to teach, and the young disdained to learn.

What was bartered for glittering trade beads? What was cast aside? Lost? Neglected? Unworthy of restoration?

If by language is meant, and I suspect that most people understand that term in its narrowest sense and application, the use of speech to communicate simple needs, simple ideas, simple sentiments and uncomplicated events such as "I'm hungry; It is round; She is lonesome," and the classic "It is raining outside," then, of course, nothing much of value is lost.

Fortunately, languages serve a higher, nobler purpose than the communication of the mundane. Winston Churchill stirred his countrymen from gloom into defiance with his speeches at the commencement of World War Two. When she felt moved to declare her love for her husband, Elizabeth Barret Browning composed "How do I love Thee," one of the finest love poems in the English speaking world. Few playwrights have entertained, enlightened and provoked audiences and readers for as long and as often as has William Shakespeare. In his efforts to draw attention to the plight of the poor and the underprivileged in order to bring about social reform, Charles Dickens wrote some of the best loved novels in the English language that added to the richness of English literature. Without the eloquent pleadings and arguments of counsel such as G.A. Martin, now a judge, J.J. Robinette and E. Greenspan to name only three, without intent to slight advocates whose names deserve to be equally acclaimed, many men and women would have been executed or sentenced to long terms in prison. In their quest for the Creator and what constituted good and what evil, humankind set down their beliefs in some of the finest passages written in their languages, The Bible, The Torah, The Koran.

It is when men and women have offered love and solace and hope, espoused right and condemned evil, chronicled their triumphs and accomplishments while admitting their defeats, failures and errors, and proclaimed their beliefs and convictions that they have enlisted language in the fulfillment of its worthiest purpose, and imparted elegance and force, grace and beauty and, in so doing, gave birth to literature.

It is in kinship to literature, its offspring, that language is to be considered and adjudged.

Beyond human calculation as is language and the literatures that it has begotten, it has incalculable worth for yet another reason.

So precious is language and the freedom that it represents that it has been granted and proclaimed as one of the rights of citizens of this country's Bill of Rights. Languages other than English or French are no less precious, and serve no less a purpose. The North American Indian languages are nothing less than the exercise of freedom and speech, and are akin to dissent in their embodiment of different ideas, opinions, perceptions, perspectives, notions, insights, institutions and understandings. Like dissent, North American Indian and other languages may serve as restraints against the ever present threat of the imposition of a single creed, ideology, or system, whether political or religious, that prefers conformity and uniformity of thought and conduct to that of diversity in opinion or practice. Where no other view or opinion or practices are tolerated, there is no freedom; and where there is no freedom, stagnation sets in.

As long as men and women can say "I have a different understanding," and are allowed to practice and exercise their political and religious beliefs, so long will knowledge and understanding grow. But the tendency has always been for institutions, governments and churches to wax larger and larger, and for its rulership and members, fearing loss of authority, power, influence, privilege and even monopoly, to suppress criticism, opposition, disagreement, news, fact and even truth. It is for these and other reasons that the Roman Catholic Church could not put up with Martin Luther or even Galileo, any more than Soviet Communism could countenance the likes of Pasternak or Solzhnitsyn. In their efforts to ensure their permanence, institutions have procreated intellectual stagnation, choked initiative, bred mediocrity and smothered hope. Only the willingness to dissent, and the good will to allow dissent, along with the resolution to uphold and defend the right, can check the tendency toward monocracy and monopoly.

And were it not for language there would be no distinction between Englishman, German, Frenchman, or a Swede; certainly the difference between them could not be deduced from the physical characteristics. It is the one feature that sets apart the Blackfoot from the Cree and the Cree from the Onondaga and the Cayuga from the Anishinaubae. Language confers an identity, a characteristic more distinctive than costume or dance or ritual. It is language that imparts upon people different values, ideals, insights, outlooks, perceptions, understandings, aspirations, institutions, and influences their customs and traditions and manners.

For a municipality to proscribe the use of a language other than the language of the majority, and for governments and institutions to undertake and to persecute the same objective by means of whips, boots, fists, rifles, abuse and ridicule, and for the natural beneficiaries of languages other than that of the country to forsake their birthright would, if such policies and procedures were successful, be a great loss, not only to the country, but to the Natives as well.

Once language and all that it represents is lost, the country may no longer have a wellspring from which to drive or borrow ideas. For example, the men and women who founded the United States modeled their constitution and government on the principles of government embodied in The Great Tree of Peace of the Five Nations Confederacy, now known as the Six Nations. And by the same token, those who have lost their ancestral language may have few new and different ideas or models that would be of service to their neighbours and strangers. They can no longer say, as did Red Jacket, the Seneca orator, "He (The Great Spirit) has given us a different understanding" and offer evidence and particulars in proof. Pontiac and Crowfoot expressed like sentiments. People who have lost their ancestral language can no longer aspire to add their heritage and culture and bequeath a legacy to their children and grandchildren. They can no longer understand, explain or interpret issues and events in terms of their cultural philosophies and institutions, but must look to others of a very different cultural background and heritage for enlightenment. Those no longer speaking the language of their forebears cannot know themselves. Unless people know themselves, know their capacities from what they have accomplished and how they fell short in the past, and have a clear purpose and destiny in mind, they cannot plot or chart their course and set their pace as truly as they ought.

A language lost is, moreover, a voice of dissent lost. While some may rejoice in the dissolution of a language, it is the country, the people, and democracy that suffers in the long run. Democracy, it is said, thrives on dissent, opposition, resistance, criticism. If this is so, then it follows that democracy suffers some attenuation when one voice of dissent is stifled. The people whose language is proscribed and hounded into oblivion suffer a greater loss in that they can no longer lend their voice to the chorus of dissent or resistance to propaganda, indoctrination, brain-washing, proselytization. With one less language, there is one less voice to cry out in protest to the imposition of a single creed, ideology, uniformity, conformity, institution, to cry out, "Enough! There is another way!"

Without language, what other characteristic is there to distinguish the Latvian from the Swede, the Dane from the Finn, or the Kutchin from the Dakota, the Dene from the Kwakiutl? What one attribute enables a man or woman to say "I am Latvian. I am a Swede. I am Kutchin. I am Dakota?" Language. And though a person has no knowledge of his ancestral tongue, yet he is not precluded from declaring "I am Anishinaubae. I am Ottawa. I am Blackfoot!" Such declarations will have as much weight as a Wayne Newton or Cher proclaiming to a nationally televised audience, "I have Cherokee blood." How much ancestral identity is lost when one is no longer in possession of that one attribute that sets his apart from other nationalities, not only in complexion but in thought, belief, perception, attitude and outlook?

Language and other languages do not receive the regard and veneration that they deserve, probably because people generally think of them, if they think of them at all, in terms of their daily experience with language that is indifferently used. It is natural and easy to take for granted, under such circumstances, that language is meant only to enable one to communicate what is in one's mind and to understand what another has said. "As long as I can say what I want, and as long as I can understand, that's all that matters" seems to sum up the general attitude toward language.

But language is more than just a means by which men and women make known their wants and needs, without regard for diction or structure or style or form. It is the means by which men and women gain and grow in knowledge, as it is the means by which they maintain their liberties and self determination, and it is the same means that impresses upon them their identities, distinguishing them from all others.

When men and women exercise their speech in the advancement of knowledge and beauty, the cause of freedom, upholding their national identity, in fostering good will, then language can never cost too much, despite what his worship, the mayor of Sault Ste. Marie, Ontario and others like him may think, and notwithstanding whatever rationale or excuse they may offer. Language, any and all languages, and the benefits they procure for humankind, are beyond price.

It is only in recent years that provincial governments have relented in their exclusion of languages other than English and French from the classroom. Under the heritage languages program, Ontario has allocated time for the teaching of North American Indian languages, and has assisted in the publication of bright, glossy, fat Curriculum Guidelines. Fine and dandy. But unless there are texts and audio broadcasts and programs of excellence available to teachers and students, then all the sheen and shine and bulk and detail of guidelines will be of little use. No. The governments need to do more. Like the Soviet Union, whether one likes it or not, the governments must assist the publication of instructional as well as literary texts, and support the efforts to preserve the North American Indian languages within Canada until such time that support is no longer necessary.

"They Didn't Teach Us Anything"

(A Proposal To Improve Native Language Teachers' Training)

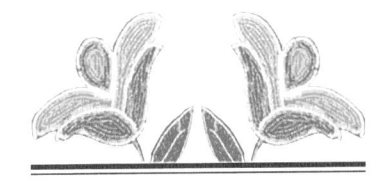

Basil H. Johnston, O.Ont., LLD., B.A. © November 1995

"They Didn't Teach Us Anything"

(A Proposal To Improve Native Language Teachers' Training)

AILMENT

Despite all the talent, money, and time that has been expended in conducting courses for teachers of Native languages and in publishing guidelines, the ultimate objectives, that of teaching students to speak their language and to prepare them to understand their cultural heritage, has not been achieved. Except for a few instances, most language courses of study have provided students with no more than lists of words.

If, after one academic year of study, students can no more understand or utter the most rudimentary statements it is because:

> 1. too little classroom time has been allotted to language instruction and study,
>
> 2. too much of the methodology based on linguistics is humdrum, boring and unimaginative,
>
> 3. too many people who do not speak a Native language and have no direct stake in the well being of a Native tongue other than a fleeting interest, set policy, publish guidelines and texts, and develop language teachers' courses and curricula,
>
> 4. too many courses have been conducted for the benefit of linguists rather than for teachers who complained that "they didn't teach us anything; we taught them," and "all we did was play sex games with words, guessing which ones were animate and inanimate," and
>
> 5. too much is expected of language students. They are expected to learn to read, write, spell, speak, understand a new language and to memorize the sex of words, all at the same time. While there are some students who may learn a language in this fashion, most do so by first understanding the spoken word, and then by enunciating it.

Is it any wonder that students get discouraged and parents complain that their children are not learning their languages?

Who ought, and who can remedy the state of Native language teacher training and Native language teaching. It is the Native peoples and Native teachers who have a direct stake in the development of their language and literature and, therefore, must provide direction in planning and setting language teacher courses, language programs, and in developing resource materials. But ultimately it is the governments, through their ministries or departments of education, who have not only the authority but also the means to improve the quality of teacher training and classroom instruction.

If the quality of Native language teacher training is to be improved, then the Native language must be regarded not in terms of morphemics, dialects, or linguistics, but rather as an element of and a means to an understanding of the cultural and spiritual heritage of the Nation. Indeed, a root may have its own gender, habitat, mood, voice, tense, sound, and may even have its own limited meaning, but only when joined with other words does it take on added meaning and begin to propagate ideas. Whatever words may be, they remain but particles in the aggregate of language. And though language may serve daily needs and practical ends, it is in the larger context of ideas, institutions, beliefs, feelings, perceptions, matters of culture, that it derives its fullest meaning and widest application.

In order to provide the kind of instruction that students deserve in order to speak their language and to appreciate their heritage, language teachers must receive, in addition to a diversified course in language teaching methodology, courses in etymology, translation, literature and history, and in the institutions and philosophy of their Nation. Students, especially older students, want to know the meaning and origin of words; they ask about the names of plants, animals, fish, reptiles and insects; they want to understand customs, rituals and ceremonies; and they are anxious to learn about beliefs and perceptions. Should a teacher repeatedly fail to provide answers or suitable explanations to questions, he or she will eventually lose the interest and confidence of the students and do a disservice to the language and the heritage. With training of greater depth and breadth than they are now receiving, teachers could better provide richer instruction to students.

REMEDIES

Methodology

There is already a considerable collection of videotaped language teaching methodology that has been developed by the Teaching English as a Second Language Association in Toronto. In the collection are some of the finest demonstrations of teaching methods and techniques. Viewing these sample lessons and mastering the principles of effective instruction will enhance Native language teachers' proficiency.

Although excellent and worthwhile, the methods demonstrated on videotapes do not provide universal application in Native languages that are, in many respects, quite unlike either English or French. To provide videotaped demonstrations of those aspects of a Native language, teachers themselves should produce such filmed lessons. In fact, it would be well worthwhile to do a series of videotaped lessons covering all aspects of language methodology in a Native language, with master teachers as producers and performers.

Etymology

The majority of Anishinaubae words may be described as "compounds," that is, words made up of affixes and core terms. It would be safe to say that it is the character of the majority of words to have two and three meanings, one bearing a common meaning, and the others senses even more fundamental than the ordinary and commonly accepted meaning. For example, "W'abi-dagooshin" is immediately understood to mean "he or she arrives". But in parsing "w'abi-dagooshin" into its basic components "abi" (here, in this place) and "dagoh" (there is, it is there, it is blended, joined, mingled, mixed, united, etc.), the terms yield a more fundamental and intrinsic meaning that may be expressed as follows: "he/she comes here to become one or united with us". One other example, "mashki-aki", would be quite enough to show the dual meaning of Anishinaubae words. The word "mashki-aki" at once and in every Anishinaubae community is understood to refer to medicine or some healing substance, but the conjunction of "mashki" (strength, power, vitality, energy, force, etc.) and "aki" (earth, land, soil, etc.) evokes the image of the earth infusing its strength and vitality into a man or woman through its plants to restore such sick person to good health and strength.

Besides providing teachers and scholars with the means of understanding the senses of words, the study of etymology may well serve as the instrument by which Anishinaubae perceptions are studied and understood. But before such a course is offered, the affixes that constitute an elemental part of words and the language must be identified and recorded, and until that is done, any attempts to resolve the orthography of the Anishinaubae language must be suspended.

Translation

As a means of nurturing greater precision and grace in the use of language, there is hardly a better exercise than translations.

Translation is the interpretation of a speech or text from one language to another which, if it is to be well done, demands of the translator a thorough knowledge not only of the language of the original speech or text, but an equal fluency in the language into which the original is to be rendered. It is a difficult art, but one that can be developed with practice and exercise.

For a person to translate faithfully as well as accurately, he or she must know syntax, grammar, idioms, figures of speech, colloquialisms, dialects, jargon, formal and informal language, ceremonies, beliefs and history. It is only by knowing grammar and tribal cultural history that a translator or scholar can go beyond the compass of literal translation to render a free translation that reflects the form, texture and mood of the original speech or text.

Quite apart from its merits as a means of training for accurate translation and interpretation, there is hardly an exercise better suited than practice in translation to develop one's writing skills. At some stage in their study of language, students must apply what they have learned in exercises of ever-increasing difficulty. In order for teachers to provide the kind of instruction and guidance that best imparts skill and fluency in writing and in diction, they themselves must receive courses in translation and interpretation.

Translation has a double advantage; it confers accuracy of expression in the original language, and such exercise imparts competency in the second language.

Literature

What people do and what they think and understand of life is embodied in their stories, myths, legends, chants, songs, the whole of which constitutes their literary and cultural heritage. It is such knowledge and understanding that a race or nation or tribe wishes to bequeath to its youth and future generations, who in turn will add to it new interpretations and applications.

Language has two ends; one is to provide men and women with the means to communicate daily matters, and the other is to articulate and understand the abstract. If Native language teachers are to instill in their students an appreciation for and an understanding of their cultural heritage, then teachers must know something of their Nation's literature.

In a very real sense the modern teacher has replaced the storyteller as trustee and executor of tribal heritage. But despite all the modern advantages available, the modern teacher has not accomplished as much as his or her predecessor.

It is said that long before the coming of books and radios and schools, tribal storytellers told stories every evening from the first fall of snow until the last flake had melted upon the ground in spring, such was their fund of knowledge of stories and powers of imagination. Much has been recorded, but much of what has been transcribed and transliterated has been denuded of its charm, humour, and substance; what remains are the skeletons of the originals. And even though a considerable portion of Anishinaubae literature may have been lost, enough remains to provide this and future generations with a general idea as to what ideals, principles, values, codes and traditions governed the conduct and inspired the thoughts of the Anishinaubae peoples; enough remains to furnish writers with themes and ideas for poetry, drama, novels, satire, humour and stories to be written with new and fresh interpretations.

For teachers to fulfill their duties in transmitting tribal traditions they must know not only the narratives but the soul, flesh, bones, arteries, sinews and heart of the stories. Training in narration and interpretation of stories should constitute a required course for teachers.

It is only by knowing the content and substance of stories, together with their features and themes, that teachers of language and literature can provide instruction that will bring intellectual growth and moral inspiration.

JUSTICE

The name Anishinaubae (Anishinaubaek in the plural) that our ancestors chose for themselves and passed down to us has a relevance that goes beyond its purpose of denoting identity or expressing a good opinion of self. It conveys the notion that human beings generally mean well, and that the fundamental goodness of human nature derives from intent. That is the understanding of human nature, and that is what the name Anishinaubae implies.

Since the notion of the essential goodness of human nature was derived from intent and the attempts to bring about the good intended, and to fulfill duties and discharge responsibilities to live by the codes, the term "Anishinaubae" implicitly encompassed human conduct, good and otherwise, and the correction of misconduct. Accordingly, the failure to achieve the good intended, or to neglect duties, or to flout the codes was seen, not as evil per se, but rather, considering the odds that humans face, as lapses, temporary losses of direction, misconduct.

When misconduct resulted in death, injury or insult that led to disputes and conflicts, the issues, if they were to be settled, were submitted to certain elders for conciliation. For the system to work, the willingness and the agreement of the victim (if still alive) and his family to forgive had to be solicited and obtained. No less crucial to the success of the mediation was the offender's agreement to ask for forgiveness and to consent to making restitution, which was tantamount to an admission of guilt. If the parties were agreeable, they were brought together to negotiate a settlement, but if no agreement to conciliate could be elicited, then exile for the offender was imposed but could not be enforced. There was, to the Anishinaubae peoples, no fate worse than ostracism; to be homeless, friendless, destined for limbo after death, shut out even from the Land of Souls.

Education

Conciliation was entrusted to and conducted by men and women thought to be the best suited to settle disputes by virtue of their common sense, judgement, knowledge, understanding, compassion, respect for traditions, kinship with the Manitous, care for their neighbours, frequency of vision, and integrity of spirit.

What these men and women were, and what they knew, was not acquired by chance or gained through personal experience, although some may have become what they were and knew what they knew in this way, but was acquired through the tutelage of elders.

Not everyone was privileged to receive the kind of tutelage as was offered by certain elders at the "Teaching Rock", Kikinoo-maugae-assin. Only those deemed deserving of such training were chosen.

But before making their choices, the Elders kept youths under observation, watching for certain traits such as solidity of character, a disposition for learning, a predilection for dreaming, and a veneration for traditions, ceremonies and the Manitous.

The instructions given to youths after their twelfth year, unlike other teachers, were more formal and were conducted in remote setting after all the snow had melted. These continued periodically until late fall. There was a practical reason for conducting such lessons in the summer months; only then were the glyphs representing the knowledge and the wisdom of the Nation accessible; at other times they were covered with snow, leaves, branches, mosses, bark and boughs that keep them concealed.

When the Elders took their protégés to the Teaching Rock, they had to uncover the glyphs etched in the face of the stone, an act symbolic of the process that takes place in teaching and learning with the tutor uncovering what has been hidden and the student seeing, hearing, sensing and feeling realities, truths, meanings that often lie unperceived below the surface of stories, words, sounds, chants, spectacles, and events in the skies. For the protégés the physical uncovering of the symbols and images, and the enlightenment that followed, was nothing less than revelation as the tutors explained the meanings of stories, chants, and words, bringing to light the underlying ideas, beliefs, codes, prophecies, perceptions, and institutions that were not immediately evident. At the end of each session the glyphs were covered over again.

Instructions continued for years. What these youths were expected to learn, to uphold and to enrich with their own insights was the cultural and spiritual heritage; and what they were expected to do was to give direction and purpose as well as a sense of worth and pride in being what they were.

These men and women were the trustees of the accumulated knowledge and wisdom of the community and the nation. By entrusting the upkeep, care, interpretation and transmission of knowledge and wisdom to men and women of character and integrity, the people were giving due recognition to the kinship that exists between knowledge and wisdom, credibility and rectitude. For knowledge to take root and flourish it had to be credible, and its bearer truthful and upright. The people urged the young to listen to them for what they knew and for what they were.

Knowledge and wisdom were precious. They had to be seeded and tilled, tended and nurtured, and safeguarded to fruition. They represented understanding and imagination, vision and hope; it was nothing less than the soul, spirit and heart of the people. Without it, the people were as nothing. They owed their all, their identity, their purpose and being, to it.

Our ancestors knew the value of an education over and above the basic skills everyone was expected to acquire and to exercise, and so they instituted instructions at Teaching Rocks.

IDEAS AND INSTITUTIONS

From such oft repeated observations as "they had no notion of private property," "they had no concept of central government," "they had no idea of human freedoms or rights," "they had no organized religion," "they had no wheel," etc., it is clear that the commentators, ecclesiastical or secular, either did not understand or, if they did understand, chose not to acknowledge the validity of Anishinaubae ideas or institutions.

Had missionaries, scholars, historians and anthropologists investigated without bias, they might have found that the Anishinaubae peoples understood both private and communal ownership, but preferred to hold that, with respect to land, ownership was vested in the nation. For the Anishinaubae nation, ownership of land was conferred by Kitchi-Manitou upon the nation; for as long as the people endure, so long will it possess title and right to the land and a claim to the yield of the land, air, and its waters. Only the nation owned the land; the nation is part of the land and cannot be regarded as separate from it. A person only had tenure during the course of his life, and a trust to care for the land and the animal-beings upon it for the benefit of the community and future generations, who in their turn will come into tenure and trust.

It is not likely that the Anishinaubaek or their Six Nations neighbours would have surrendered their personal freedom, or readily submitted to authority. Such was their conviction of their intrinsic worth and equality that the Anishinaubae peoples seldom deferred to naked authority, or yielded their independence, or entrusted their well being to another except on special occasions, and only for brief periods. In Anishinaubae eyes, no man or woman was better than his brothers or sisters. To this day the Anishinaubae peoples' conviction in equality of worth remains as firm as it has always been, and their resentment of any intrusion upon their independence through the exercise of authority has not abated.

Action and wisdom and accountability were the stuff of men and women, chiefs and councillors. Next to deeds, what the Anishinaubaek most respected was speech. Perhaps the Kiowa author and Pulitzer prize winner, Scott Momaday, best expressed his tribe's regard for language: "Words were medicine; they were magic and invisible. They came from nothing into sound and meaning. They were beyond price; they could neither be bought nor sold...." To the Anishinaubaek and other nations, words were no less medicinal. To us they were medicine and sacred, bad and good; they could either injure or heal, offend or comfort, mislead or enlighten. And insofar as words move or inform, they are the creations of the speaker, reflecting his or her moods, sentiments and skill with ideas. And just as the medicine man or woman can heal only as much as his limited powers allow, so a speaker can impart only what is within his knowledge, and articulate only what is within his command of language.

Much work and study remains to be done in order to understand Anishinaubae ideas and institutions. Until that study is done, the Anishinaubae peoples and their teachers cannot fully understand the philosophy or the philosophic basis for their institutions, ceremonies, rituals, customs and beliefs and, not in full command of the cultural ideas and institutions, cannot fully transmit them to their children. In the meantime, the Anishinaubae peoples must rely upon West European texts and authorities for information and interpretation concerning their heritage, and continue to teach their heritage in terms of canoe construction, food preparation, clothing styles, and subsistence patterns as if Anishinaubae institutions either did not exist, or if they did exit, had neither merit nor validity.

BENEFITS

If such courses as are recommended in this proposal are implemented, they will yield at least four benefits.

For Ministries and Departments of Education and universities, implementation will enhance the quality of their curricula and guidelines and courses.

For teachers there would be a better appreciation of the nature and character of their Native language, along with a firmer grasp of their literary and cultural heritage, resulting in personal growth. And with a broader background in methodology, combined with sounder scholarship, language teachers will be better prepared to conduct classes and courses with greater imagination.

But it will be students, elementary, secondary, undergraduate and graduate, who will have most to gain. For, in addition to learning to speak their Native language, they will also learn about their literature and institutions.

I ALWAYS WANTED TO BE AN INDIAN

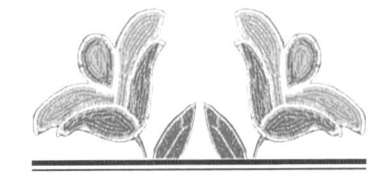

BASIL H. JOHNSTON, O.ONT., LLD., B.A. © 1995

THINK INDIAN

I ALWAYS WANTED TO BE AN INDIAN

In 1968 I was invited to an Indian display mounted by the grade five students of Churchill Avenue Public School in North York as a grand finale to their five-week in-depth study of Indians. Students, parents and teachers were justifiably proud of the exhibition.

The entire library was one large, open gallery. It was a veritable feast of Native memorabilia. Against the walls were tables bearing an array of pictures, maps and artifacts, both genuine and plastic. Posters and several large pictures of Indian chiefs and warriors adorned the walls. At one end of the library was a large canvas teepee; in front a tripod made of saplings meant to represent an outdoor fireplace. Students, whose faces were painted in warlike colours and wearing paper headdresses, mingled with the guests whom they conducted about the exhibits explaining what they knew of their respective First Nations. All of them wore nameplates of the tribes whom they represented: ALGONQUIN, IROQUOIS, SIOUX, HURON, OJIBWAY. In front of the teepee stood a grim-looking grade five chief, his arms folded. Like the rest of the Indians, his face was painted in hostile colours. I went directly to him.

"How!" I said in greeting.

The Blackfoot chief looked at me quizzically.

"Why so glum, chief?" I asked.

Before replying, the chief looked around to make sure that there were no teachers within hearing, and then whispered "I'm bored."

"How so, chief?"

"Sir! Don't tell anybody, but I'm bored. I'm tired of Indians. You see, sir, I always wanted to be an Indian, and when we started this unit on Indians I thought I'd learn something. When we began this unit we had to choose a special project from social organization, hunting and fishing, food preparation, clothing, dwellings, and transportation. I chose dwellings," and at this point the little chief exhaled in exasperation, "and that's all me and my committee did for five weeks, sir! We studied and researched teepees, igloos, longhouses, lodges, wigwams. We read books, encyclopedias, went to the library, looked at pictures and drew sketches. Then we had to make a teepee. Is that all there is to Indians sir?"

Two comments hit home. "Is that all there is?" and "I always wanted to be an Indian" affected me enormously and profoundly. Now there is nothing particularly unusual about wanting to be an Indian. In fact, back in the '60's a youngster aspiring to be an Indian was as common as wanting to become a fireman, policeman, nurse or actress. And children could not give a rational reason for wanting to be an Indian. It was the mystique, perhaps a romantic notion derived from a picture that attracted "Wanna-be Indians."

That youngster had a dream, preposterous as it may seem to adults, worth pursuing because it represented something real. And dreams and visions are necessary to create and to accomplish. When his school offered a five week in-depth study on Indians, that boy looked forward to the program that would teach him all he wanted to know and needed to know that would enable him to turn his dream into reality; to become a living, breathing Indian. But the course let him down. He learned about social organizations, subsistence, food, fashion, dwellings, and migration. But he uncovered nothing about the true nature of Indians. He was exasperated. Despite his disappointment, he still clung to hope. His question and tone pleaded for some assurance that "Indians" were so much more, and that it was still worthwhile to dream.

His plea was reminiscent of another boy's plea to Joe Jackson, one of the Chicago White Sox baseball players accused of deliberately losing games in the 1918 World Series to "Say it ain't so, Joe." Faith had to be restored.

To long to be an Indian, as this youngster longed to be, may be dismissed as nothing more than a childhood fancy, a phase. But the longing to be an "Indian" is not confined to youth today.

When Columbus and other European traders bound for the Orient in quest of silver, spices and silk chanced upon this continent they saw, besides land and abundance, people and customs that they had never imagined existed. The customs and the unique way of living of the brown skinned people who inhabited this continent captured their attention. The peoples of this new world could come and go as they pleased; no need to ask permission of some person of higher authority or standing; they saw these people sit, stand, eat and talk with their leaders without servility; men and women kept the fruits of their labours for their own needs, and even shared them with the needy; they saw men and women pray and worship in their own way whenever they saw the need to do so and wherever they happened to be, without the supervision or direction of a body of clergy; and they saw men and women in possession and occupation of homesteads on lands that they had chosen for themselves as their own and which their neighbours acknowledged as belonging to them. To the intruders, these customs and institutions were quite backward, primitive, uncivilized.

What these traders and adventurers observed was utterly foreign to their heritage and traditions. Where they came from men and women were serfs, servants, peasants, villeins, bondsmen, vassals and chattels who could not come and go as they pleased, or leave their master's domain and service without asking permission. Such a thing was unheard of. Most of European society was divided into classes, the upper and the lower, the former consisting of the royalty, nobility, and the clergy, and the latter of men and women of low birth and inferior status. All communication and interaction between the upper and lower classes called for the lower classes to acknowledge the superiority of the upper class. Members of the lower classes could not address members of the upper classes without first being addressed. Acts of subservience such as genuflecting in the presence of and kissing the hand of a high born were the rule. Peasants, serfs and chattels had to surrender a portion of the fruits of their labour to their masters, leaving just enough to subsist upon till the next spring. What produce these classes surrendered to their betters represented a fee for their occupation and tillage of land held by a noble on behalf of the monarch. There was no such institution as private property in land. Everything belonged to the monarch and nobility, as did everything else by virtue of the Divine Right of Kings.

Europeans believed that the Creator had bestowed all power and dominion over all land and life directly and exclusively to a monarch. Men and women all professed similar beliefs, and worshipped in churches as congregations at set times under the ministry of a clergyman. With no freedom, no equality, no prospects, men could not dream; the only ones who dared dream were young women who yearned for a prince to rescue them from their wretched hovels, or for a fairy godmother to transform their rags into gowns with a wave of her magic wand. With such heritage another way of life was inconceivable to imagine.

The traders and adventurers who happened upon lands to the south saw peoples and wonders that must have left them gasping; cities such as Tenochtitlan, highways, aqueducts, exotic fruits and vegetables, markets, plazas, squares, garments, sculptures, art, astronomy, cleanliness, gems and gold; wealth that made them all forget the Far East with its silks, spices, and silver.

On their return to their homes from the new world, these European traders and adventurers, along with their crews and recruits, described the people, the lands, the bounty, and the customs that they had observed. The traders and captains of these expeditions reported to their monarchs that they had "discovered" new lands which they had claimed on behalf of their kings and queens. The audience was skeptical of these accounts. They sounded like fairy tales. Still, as fantastic as were the reports, men and women secretly hoped that such a world existed. They hoped for a world and life far better than their own, which Jean Jacques Rousseau epitomized as no different from that of slavery in the unforgettable opening sentence to his classic work, The Social Contract, "Man is born free but everywhere he is in chains."

The monarchs, anxious to consolidate and give legitimacy to their newly arrogated dominions, and to discourage avaricious rival kings and queens from encroaching upon their latest acquisitions, sent garrisons and settlers to occupy the new territories. They even appealed to the Vatican to settle their disputes over boundaries and to declare the appropriation of territories in the Land of the Great Turtle from the legitimate and original owners and occupants of the land as ethical, moral, right, just and lawful. The Vatican obliged. Shipload after shipload of settlers came, lured by the promise of grants of land and the prospect of a life far better than what they had known or would ever know in Europe. The claims of English, Spanish, French and Portuguese monarchs were consolidated.

But while settlers and colonists came over to escape the economic and social conditions in Europe, and to make a better life in America, they brought with them beliefs, institutions, customs, traditions, habits, practices, the trappings spawned by feudal systems in Europe, and the Doctrine of the Divine Right of Kings that had contributed to their bondage. They also brought diseases.

And much as some might have wished to cast them off, the settlers and colonists were not ready to discard their chains; they were still too attached to and bound by the old regime and social order to assume something new, different and unfamiliar. But as the pioneers pushed into the interior, they experienced more and more the freedom and equality the Indians had introduced to them. And once they began to pursue their dreams, never more would they be satisfied or content with less. Never would they be comfortable as subjects of a monarch or as servants of some master.

At the outset few of the early European settlers thought of changing the status quo. As the years passed, however, these men and women lost trust and confidence in their traditional form of government. The government in London blundered and dithered in implementing its policies, interfered in the internal and domestic affairs of the colonies, impeded growth and progress, and imposed more and more taxes, the very thing the colonists had tried to escape.

The colonists became less willing to accept decisions made from across the ocean. From their homes and businesses on this side of the Atlantic, the transplanted Europeans became less certain of the old European political and social order, and more sure of their own autonomy.

They yearned for freedom, equality, independence, things that their traditions could not provide. They wanted to come and go, to stand beside other men and women as equals, to have their counsels heard and heeded by their leaders, and to pursue and practice their religious convictions and beliefs in their own way. They had to amalgamate these institutions into the social and political fabric and within a framework of law and justice similar to their West European heritage.

Despite the growing skepticism of the virtues of the old system and social structure on the part of ordinary men and women, the status quo had powerful advocates and champions in the upper classes, the established religions, and the armed forces. In one of the great ironies of history, the missionaries and later the colonial and Indian agency systems, thrust the virtues and beliefs of civilization and Christianity then prevailing in Europe upon American Indians, while many colonists were thinking of and straining to break the constraints that shackled them to the old social and political order of civilized Europe. Missionaries were particularly diligent in promoting religion, as well as championing the cause of the old order as exemplified in Europe. As the missionaries went into the interior of the continent well ahead of civilization, they invited and cajoled the Natives to renounce their sinful superstitions, beliefs, and primitive ways, and to espouse Christianity and civilization. The rewards and benefits, they told the Natives, would be inestimable. Many accepted the invitation; others did not. In declining the missionaries' invitation to convert on behalf of his people, Red Jacket, the celebrated Seneca orator, told them "the Great Spirit has given us a different understanding;" they were unwilling to repudiate what the Creator had given them. Even though Red Jacket delivered his reply on behalf of the Six Nations peoples, he expressed sentiments held by most, if not all other North American Natives. On the one hand, North American Indians were being asked in the name of Christianity and civilization to surrender their freedom, independence, equality, beliefs, institutions and land; on the other, the immigrants strained to break the bonds that shackled them to a feudal system with all its strictures and social ranks, and to established religion.

Until they chanced upon the Land of The Great Turtle, Europeans could not dream. It was only after they saw the ancestors of the Native people exercising freedoms that the colonists began to dream. They dreamed of change, and the dream gave them purpose and resolution.

It was not an easy task for missionaries or the governing officials to convince the Native peoples to accept both Christianity and civilization. Nor was it easy for them to keep their flocks and constituents from bolting orthodox religious beliefs and practices, and espousing alien and primitive values and institutions.

But the cause was already lost; it was just a question of time. It is not an easy matter for people to cast off their chains. Instead, great changes are accompanied by bloodshed. Though they had legitimate grievances that mounted every year, the colonists had no precedent to follow or model to copy in their West European heritage, advanced and cultured as it was. They needed something to guide them in establishing a new and different social and political order and system that would reflect, represent and bring about their aspirations.

Two centuries passed before these immigrants gathered their courage and cried "Hold! Hold!" A challenge was issued to their mother country, England, then one of the most powerful countries in the world. No longer would they tolerate interference from London, England, regarded as incompetent management of their affairs. It was galling to have to pay taxes and more taxes to support the British army whose presence was seen as an occupation force, and to have to provide billets to its personnel on demand. The colonists were embittered by the authority of officers of the Crown in the name of a far-off king to arrest, seize and imprison any person and to hold his property and chattels without a warrant.

In 1765 they refused to pay the Stamp Tax. Two years later, 1767, they would not pay the Townshend duties. Bolder they grew. One night in 1773, disguised as Indians, faces streaked with war paint and wielding war clubs, the malcontents boarded British vessels and dumped a cargo of tea in Boston Harbour. They refused to pay taxes for the tea.

Presumably the war party celebrated a victory dance afterward. It was only fitting that these historic protesters were disguised as Indians. It was symbolic of their frustrations and aspirations to make The Great White Father overseas take notice and listen. But nothing changed.

Finally, on the 19th of April 1775, rebels fired a shot that was heard around the world. The revolution was on.

Whether the rebellious colonists were presumptuous or confident, or both, the leaders of the uprising, with Thomas Jefferson as the chief author, drafted the Declaration of Independence that was adopted on the 4th of July, 1776.

In the very first paragraph of this document was set for the first time in writing what the North American Indians had been exercising, and what all of humanity had been endowed with: "We hold these truths to be self-evident that all men are created equal, that they are endowed by their Creator with certain alienable Rights, that among these are Life, Liberty, and the

THINK INDIAN

pursuit of Happiness." This sentence said it all.

With this declaration the colonists defied the Imperial government and repudiated the old social system, and in so doing proclaimed the freedoms and rights that all humankind is endowed with and entitled to by virtue of birth and life.

At last, after two centuries, the colonists fulfilled the dreams that had eluded their ancestors. They finally acquired by war what our ancestors, the North American Indians, had as a matter of birthright: freedom, equality, independence, land and aspiration for dream. By their revolution the Americans also set a precedent for other nations to follow; within sixteen years the people of France rose up against their monarchs and the old regime in the French Revolution, seeking "Liberté, Egalité, Fraternité." The idea and inspiration to overthrow the old order and to establish a new came not from Europe but from the Land of The Great Turtle.

In establishing a government and framing a constitution that would most accurately represent and uphold the inalienable rights of its citizens, and nourish their pursuits and aspirations, the architects of the new Republic and the authors of the Constitution had a rich legacy of political theory and practice to draw from their West European heritage. Nevertheless, they studied and adopted many of the features and principles of government and administration as embodied in The Great Tree of Peace of The Five Nations Confederacy, now the Six Nations. North American Indian notions, concepts and principles of political confederacy were adopted and amalgamated with West European in the form of government and constitution of the new Republic.

The ancestors of the citizens of the United States, Canada, Mexico, Brazil and the other nations of Central and South America were seeking a short cut to the Far East, with its treasures, silver, silk, and spices, when they chanced upon the shores of The Land of The Great Turtle. What they found here was infinitely more valuable and fulfilling than what they had been seeking. They could come and go without asking permission of a master; they could talk to officials without servility; keep the produce of their labours, dream and fulfill their dreams. They had no further need to go to the Far East. And it was the North American Indian who inspired them. It was the Indians who gave them far more than land.

You Can't Tell Stories in the Summer

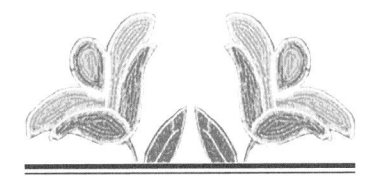

Basil H. Johnston, O.Ont., LLD., B.A. © 1998

You Can't Tell Stories In The Summer

"You can't tell stories in the summer! ... only when there's snow on the ground. Even if it's winter and there's no snow on the ground, storytellers aren't allowed to tell stories. There's gotta be snow" so say many North American Indian watchdogs living in the snow-belt, in explaining tribal storytelling practices. They don't say so in so many words, but the inference drawn from these declarations is that storytelling while flowers are in full bloom and the warblers are chirping and warbling, is a blasphemous act as reprehensible as is the eating of unkoshered meat in Jewish society. It's a terrible, sacrilegious thing to do. Orthodox traditional Indians don't do it. And people listen and wag their heads in awe at such strict compliance with the Indian Canon Law of Native storytelling. Such dedication!

But ask these safe-guardians who vouch that stories are to be told only so long as snow blankets the countryside what their source of authority is for the doctrine that they are expounding, what stories specifically recount and explain why storytelling is disallowed in the summer? What rituals? What punishments will befall the offender? Will the Manitous unleash bolts of lightning to strike the errant storyteller dumb or dead for breaking one of the storytelling commandments? Will neighbours banish the misguided storyteller from their midst to wander abroad homeless, friendless and familyless as they once did unrepentant murderers?

Ask these self-appointed custodians of the sanctity of storytelling these questions. None will be able to tell you where the commandment "Thou shalt not tell stories so long as the ground is snowless" came from or why it is in force. Few can speak the ancestral language, or are acquainted with more than half a dozen stories. And yet they are loud and adamant in proclaiming that storytelling in the summer is forbidden; a No! No!

When I first heard of this restriction more than 30 years ago, I checked with Mrs. Jane Rivers from the Wikemikong Indian Reserve, an old dear friend, now deceased, whether story-telling in the summer months was forbidden, and what would happen to a person breaking the commandment. She too had heard about the restriction, but didn't know whether it was true or not; and, so far as she knew, the worst fate that a storyteller might suffer was to dream of a frog or receive a visit from a real frog. For some, the apparition of a frog, a terrifying experience in itself, was an omen of worse things to come. Mrs. Rivers smiled as she envisioned this horrific ordeal. Pauline Pelley of Saskatchewan gave me a similar explanation.

Over the years I have found nothing in traditional stories that forbids storytelling in the snowless season. From the absence of any word in stories forbidding the telling of stories in summer, it is safe to assume that the belief that storytelling is a winter-only exercise is a recent development.

To accept the opinion that storytelling is permissible only during the snow-bound season comes from a misunderstanding of stories and storytelling.

There is nothing mysterious about the purpose of storytelling. It is meant to teach and to amuse; nothing more, nothing less. Storytellers tell stories to open minds and to cheer and uplift the hearts and spirits of their listeners. If they can open minds and draw smiles in the same story, they have done something. Listeners came to storytelling sessions not only to pass the time away during the long winter evenings, but to learn something of their history, traditions, customs, beliefs, rituals, codes, the manitous, the other world, the after-life, the before-life, language, medicine, zoology, botany, geography, songs, dreams, and some simply to laugh. Storytelling is meant to teach.

The young want to know. They need to know. The old have what youth needs to know, and the old need to pass on what they know. It was by listening that youth grew in mind, heart, soul, and spirit. And as individuals grow, so does the nation's store of knowledge and its sense of worth and purpose.

The want and need to know begin at birth, and continue day after day, week after week, month after month, year after year, until death. The desire and the need to know are not subject to schedule or controlled by closed and open seasons. Storytelling and teaching must be ever ready to fulfill the demands for knowledge whenever it is received, snow or no snow.

Our ancestors understood this principle of teaching and learning, and they taught when the occasion and the necessity to do so arose, not when taboos, if such there were, dictated when it was permissible to do so.

Neither children nor their need of want to know are set by some timetable, any more than events, accidents or incidents occur according to a master plan. Thunderstorms, meteor showers, lightning, northern lights, plagues of tent caterpillars and earthquakes take place at no given time, and their occurrence prompts questions that demand answers and explanations as they occur, not later.

Parents and grandparents never know when their children will misbehave; parents and grandparents must keep their eyes and their ears on the unexpected.

With children, it's not likely that even God knows what they'll do next. One moment they're like angels, the next like little hellions. They fight, they tease, they lose their moccasins, they want this and that, they want their playmate's toy, they want their playmate's food. They play too near the fireplace. They go farther out into the lake than is wise. They kick the dog or pull its tail. They catch frogs and salamanders who they prod with sticks or stretch.

When children act like hellions or hooligans, their grandparents, but chiefly their grandmothers, set them straight as to what was right and what was wrong by telling them stories then and there. As usual, there were the age-old reprimands screamed or shouted, "Don't! Don't do that! Stop it! You'll get hurt! You'll get burned! You'll poke your eye out! You'll hurt someone!"

Commands, "Don't do that! You'll get hurt!", no matter how often or angrily bellowed, seldom gain instant or long-lasting compliance. Usually the admonitions go through one ear and out the other, and are forgotten. Explanations, rational and logical, bring nods of understanding and promises of "I won't do it again!" but soon pass out of mind into the unremembered past.

Parents and grandparents knew that negative commandments consisting of "Thou Shalt Not …" were not as effective as stories in dealing with behaviour. Stories drawn from real life experiences that dramatized the price of misbehaviour, mistake, neglect, blunder, oversight, misunderstanding, carelessness, disobedience, impulsiveness or giving hurt, lingered longer in memories, and in some instances brought about an improvement in behaviour.

Parents dealt with misdeeds performed by their offspring in the summer in the same way as they dealt with the ones committed in the winter. They dealt with them at once. They scolded. They told a story to illustrate what they meant.

Mischief and delinquency were but two instances that called for teaching and storytelling. For a community and society to grow, it is imperative that its knowledge and experiences be passed on. Our Anishinaubae ancestors kept records of its spiritual and intellectual teachings and understandings engraved on rocks, or etched on birchbark scrolls that were stored in sealed caves that were accessible only in the summer months. Only when the ground was bare, covered with grasses and flowers and leaves that had replaced the snow were instructions given. Only then could the Elders, accredited as custodians of the heritage, and as men and women abiding by the great laws, take especially selected youngsters to these places of instruction, known as Kikinoomaugae-assin (The Teaching Rocks) where, reading from the glyphs, they passed on what they knew and understood of their history, beliefs, institutions, customs, traditions, prophecies, chants (psalms), dreams, insights, outlooks, the manitous, life, the after-life, and human conduct. The tutors told stories to their protégés who one day would succeed them as Elders whose advice and guidance were worth listening to and following.

The Elder-mentors, trained as such, instilled in their protégés not only knowledge but a respect for life and learning that conferred credibility and lent weight to their teachings and to their roles as teachers, arbiters, and conciliators.

To say that stories are to be told only in summer gives the impression that Anishinaubae storytellers are hide-bound in following all the trumped-up rules that govern storytelling, and that they still hold court as they once did throughout the winter evenings. But, sad to say, storytelling and listening has gone out of fashion, the way that many customs have gone; it is no longer the principal source of teaching and learning and entertainment in First Nations homes. Storytelling has been supplanted by television, bingo, radio, video, books. Storytellers have a smaller stock of stories to narrate; they have fewer opportunities to practice their art, except on special occasions when they are invited to entertain students or audiences on Indian Awareness Days or at conferences. Storytelling sessions, as once conducted in every Anishinaubae community, are just memories that are recalled as "Our storytellers used to…." There is not even an evening set aside for this practice. And no one can recall when Elders last took youth to the teaching rocks to teach them how to "Think Indian." In recent years, the Teaching Rocks have been declared "Historic Sites," preserved under glass and offered as a museum artifact for the benefit of tourists to photograph and later to discuss with their acquaintances in terms of their interest.

"You can't tell stories in the summer" is misleading, having no foundation in practice or in need. It may well be an excuse for the growing lack of knowledge of the ancestral languages, traditions, storytelling and the purpose of stories in life.

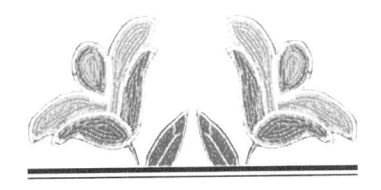

INDIAN IDENTITY

WHO ARE WE?

BASIL H. JOHNSTON, O.ONT., LLD., B.A. © 1998

THINK INDIAN

Indian Identity

Who are we?

Last autumn the Indians in and around San Francisco forced the enemy to bite the dust and to surrender their arms by making a treaty in which all the ball teams in the area bearing the name of Indians or of a specific tribe agreed to knock off the practice. The names and logos were insulting to the North American Natives, The Bay warriors chanted. Yielding to pressure, The Bay school teams complied. They removed the offending names from their caps, jackets, uniforms. No more "Indians," "Apaches," "Comanches." They were history, to be remembered only in history books and museums and at pow-wows.

What led to this and similar demands made of the Cleveland, Washington, Atlanta, Chicago and other athletic clubs in recent years? When asked, North American Indians invariably answer, "We're not INDIANS! We're not from INDIA! The team names and logos are offensive. We're not REDSKIN!... and that Chief Wahoo!... it ridicules us."

And I suppose there is some merit in all these objections. We are not from the country shown as India on the maps. And I have grave doubts that the people of so-called "India" refer to themselves as "Indians." Nor are we red-skinned as we are sometimes depicted, but shaded in all tones of brown and copper. What could have led to the rise of the term "Redskin" was the practice of some of our ancestors to paint their faces and bodies with ochre on occasion. Or a colour blind person mistaking brown for red could have easily conferred the name on us. As for "Chief Wahoo," I concede that it may offend certain sensitivities, but he sure reminds me of certain chiefs, councillors and other Indians whom I've known.

If North American Indians have not received the respect they crave and deserve they shouldn't place all the blame on baseball, football, or hockey clubs. Historians, clergymen, ethnologists, anthropologists, archaeologists and teachers may be more at fault for the image that citizens of the U.S.A. and Canada have of us.

THINK INDIAN

Native demands for ball clubs to discontinue their use of misleading names and tasteless logos is, underneath, a plea for acceptance as equals with the other citizens of these two countries.

But the real reason for North American Indian objection to these ball clubs using Indian names and logos is, I suspect, that by losing more often than winning, these teams give all of us a bad image, that of losers. Born to lose, destined to lose. For the clamours for these ball clubs to stop abusing Indian names is loudest when Cleveland, Atlanta and Washington are losing; hardly a peep when they're winning.

The past few years have been pretty good years for the Indian image … for Indians. Nobody minded the name "Indian," "Redskin" or "Brave" too much; few were offended by Chief Wahoo. It was intoxicating to read "Indians Wallop Yankees," "Braves rout Texas Rangers," "Redskins massacre Patriots." Far better than "Indians lose another one," "Braves clobbered," "Redskins thrashed." Yes, one couldn't be too put out with Chief Wahoo for smirking at the squirming enemy.

I like Wahoo. He's a happy Indian, win or lose. He can grin in triumph; he can grin in defeat: "you got me this time, but my day is coming; better watch your goddam wagons." Wahoo may not be as handsome as some would like him to be, but that's not Wahoo's fault, any more than it's the Cleveland Indian baseball club's fault. Blame the Indian who posed for the ball club's promotion and publicity department: buck toothed, hook nosed and moon-eyed. I'm sure that the Cleveland Indians baseball club would lend a willing ear to proposals to replace Wahoo with a good looking Ojibway, even of teeth, straight of nose, and regular of eye, a no nonsense Indian, stoic like 'Kaw-Liga'. But changing the logo with a fresh Indian, say Tom Jackson or Graham Greene, just wouldn't cut the mustard. They're not the types to gloat after having beaten the hell out of a Beantowner.

The parades and marches, with placards and chants demanding that the ball clubs cease slighting North American Indians and their cultures would be worthwhile demonstrations if the Indians who are the most vociferous paid as much respect for their heritage by learning to speak their Native language and knowing something of their cultures as they are demanding of others.

THINK INDIAN

Sad to say, most of the protesters have made little or no attempt to learn the language of their ancestors and so perpetuate their heritage. There is no better way of showing one's love for one's heritage than by speaking the language. Better that these protesters spend their efforts and energies learning their language and traditions than engaging in tub thumping for a better image. Knowing who they are will make it easier for them to put up with mistaken identities.

As one North American Indian wit advised, "Don't be too offended by the name 'Indian;' it isn't as bad as what you think. Just thank Kitchi-Manitou that these guys weren't looking for Turkey."

After these peddlers got lost and ran aground on this continent, believing that it was India and calling our people Indians, they settled here. They claimed that they discovered the continent and the people on it, and explored it. This continent that the West Europeans called the New World wasn't lost, nor was it new. It was as old as the Old World, already settled and well known to the people and the animals that lived here. And De Soto, Cortes, Champlain, La Salle and all the rest didn't explore or find anything as they claimed and are credited with by historians. The land, every lake, river, forest, mountain range, marsh, was already well known to our ancestors, who conducted these adventurers westward into the interior along travel routes well known and well established. But it was just in keeping with these people to take all the credit, never mind giving any due to their guides who already knew the way and who knew where to camp, how to hunt and what to eat. Without our ancestors to guide them, these adventurers would have perished.

These West Europeans were curious about us "Indians." They wanted to know who our ancestors were and what they were doing on this continent, as if our ancestors didn't belong here. But it never occurred to the West Europeans to question the origin of the buffaloes or butterflies. These people finally decided that our ancestors were of the Mongoloid race, kin to Chinese, Japanese, Tibetans, Koreans. Bingo, our ancestors were Indians, of the Mongoloid race, their origins elsewhere but on the continent.

But that was just for starters. To be fully understood we had to be classified, for that is the civilized, learned way. Everything, every creature, plant, belongs to a class, known by a Greek term. Indians, Mongoloids, had to belong to some category.

After prolonged study, anthros (anthropologists hate the term), ethnologists, archaeologists began their scientific, systematic classification of the "Indigenous" peoples of the Americas. ARCTIC. SUB-ARCTIC, then, for some inexplicable reason, dropped these climatic, zonal classifications which logically they should have continued to its logical end. They would have come up with some beauts: SUB-SUB-ARCTIC, MID-TEMPERATE, TEMPERATE, SEMI-TROPICAL, TROPICS, so on and so forth. Teachers would have introduced a unit on Indians: "Today we're going to study 'Temperate Indians'." But these scholars changed "canoes in midstream" as our ancestors might have said. After SUB-ARCTIC they opted for topographical terminology: WOODLANDS, PLAINS, COASTAL. Then they changed canoes again, going for orientational terms: SOUTHWEST Indians, SOUTHEAST Indians.

To know that an Indian was SUB-ARCTIC, PLAINS or SOUTHEAST immediately revealed a great deal about them.

The one that I, and many of us, belong to is "WOODLAND." Right off it reminds me of the illustrations of our ancestors, and the descriptions of their way of life. Bushy Indians skulking behind trees, dancing in a glade, sitting around a fireplace listening to fireside stories. They hunted, they are nomadic, they are children of nature; they are very spiritual. To some they were savages. Hell, if they were as savage as they were made out to be, Champlain, Cartier and all those sedentary characters would have been bludgeoned and butchered and discovered either Heaven or Hell; they would never have lived to tell any tales. And the "authorities" wrote that our ancestors dropped rocks in containers to make stews, soups and various beverages.

Sad to say, but our own schools use these books as texts in their courses of study. They perpetuate the myth that our grandmothers had a large pile of stones beside a large pile of firewood, next to the central fireplace, and that they had wooden tongs with which to immerse and extract the stones until the broth was done, without leaving ash and grit in the broth. Have the authors or teachers never given this manner of cooking some thought, or conducted an experiment to determine whether the process works and how long it would take to boil soup or tenderize Indian corn or reduce sap to syrup and then on to sugar? Just try to imagine how long it would take to boil maple sap to a syrupy state. Yet our teachers blithely teach this stuff.

The clues that our Bushy ancestors had containers in which to boil water, stews, broths and medicinal beverages are to be found in the language. Take the work "akik," a vessel made from the earth, earthenware or a clay pot or urn. Properly glazed and set over coals, a clay pot can be used to heat and boil water. And water can be brought to a boil in a birch bark container called piskitae-naugun. There was no need for cooks to bobble stones around in some container and afterwards have diners spit out grit and ash, or crack their teeth.

Our ancestors may have been backward in many respects, but they knew something about the preparation of foods and virtue of conserving time.

Some years ago, after I was done doing a take-off on the designations Woodland and Bushy, a young man from the Couchiching Reserve in Northwestern Ontario observed, "Sir! With the logging outfits clear-cutting all the forests, I guess we should be called CLEAR-CUTS" ... and I suppose we should.

And of course the linguists, bless their little tongues, got into the act, carving the Indians into linguistic slices: Algonkian, or is it Algonquin?, Hidatsan, Souian, Dene, Haidan, so on and so forth. By the time these people got done, our ancestors and our generation was reeling with identities. Once just Anishinaubaek, Mongoloid, or Asiatic, Ojibwa, Ojibway or Chippewa, a Woodland Indian of the Algonkian, or is it Algonquin? stock, or is it linguistic group?

Our ancestors took unto themselves the name Anishinaubae, the Good-beings, to reflect their opinion of themselves. Now scholars and academics were telling us what we were and what language group we belong to, and these people not only could not get the spellings consistent, but they screwed up meanings as well, translating Ojibway, or is it Chippewa?, as meaning "those who wear puckered up moccasins." People, no matter where in the world, took names for themselves that projected a good image of themselves, not for public relations but from a simple pride in who they were, not from some article of clothing that tells nothing of what people think of themselves. Our ancestors were no different; they thought well of themselves.

It was our kin, the "Cree," a name not of their choosing either, who gave us the name, a term mildly disparaging of our manner and style of speech.

THINK INDIAN

We all speak at a faster rate than our kin, the Cree, but our Manitoulin Island brothers and sisters take the prize for speaking at machine gun rapidity. We have abbreviated many of our words. Wikwemikong will soon be replaced by Wiky; kitchi is chi; ginae-beeg is naybig. There are hundreds of other monstrosities. No wonder the Cree called us "Chippewae," the people who sound funny, stuttering and stammering as they talk.

Now we were a sub-group of the Algonkian, or is it Algonquin?, linguistic group. What the term meant none of the scholars could say because none of them ever bothered to learn one of the Native languages. My fellow Anishinaubaek, when asked, shook their heads. They didn't know that, in addition to being Sub-Arctic, Woodland, Ojibway, they were Algonkian. Books were of no help. Not even the so-called Algonquin of Maniwaki, Quebec, who referred to themselves as "Maumeek," knew the origin or the meaning of the word. And as an "Algonkian" it bugged me not to know what I was.

In 1985 I was invited to take part in a weekend seminar as a speaker, conducted by the Lansing, Michigan Indian Club parents for the benefit of their children on Michillimackinac Island.

One of the first people to greet me on my arrival was Joe Migwanibi of Hannaville, Michigan. I had not seen Joe since we were both in Residential School in Spanish, Ontario, some 45 years earlier. Joe had become an accomplished storyteller, and he was in a storytelling mood; on a roll.

"You know what Algonquin means?" he asked me.

"No" I confessed.

"Wanna know what it means?"

"I'll die a happier death."

It was as if the fates had at last wanted me to know.

"It's a long story," Joe began, "but I'll shorten it; it all started the very first winter that the Pale Faces spent here. They didn't bring any winter clothing with them, so sure were they that they would get to India where never was seen a flake of snow or chill penetrate the marrow of Indian.

Well, these peddlers were soon freezing their buns off with their thin underwear, pants, shirts, coats, hats, silk dresses, sheer stockings, leather shoes, and handkerchiefs. They didn't have proper heating in the houses they built; they didn't have warm blanketing or bedding, or know how to keep a fire going. They didn't even know the difference between poplar and pine. As for food, they wouldn't eat our foods but stuck to salt pork, salt fish and cabbages. No wonder they got sick.

Our ancestors felt sorry for these people. They brought them medicine, warm clothing made of buckskin, jackets, leggings, moccasins, hats, mitts and warm bedding made of bearskin and rabbit.

When these people went back to where they came from the following spring for more trade goods, some of them took, as souvenirs, the clothing that our ancestors had given them to show their friends at home.

A revolution occurred, one of many to take place in civilized Europe after our ancestors and the Pale Faces met. Our beaver hats captured the fancy of the fashion conscious ladies of high birth, like you wouldn't believe. The men too caught the fever. On the next trip the Pale Face peddlers asked our ancestors to supply any quantity of beaver pelts that they might require for their kin in Europe. Soon there were orders for the purchase of all the beaver pelts that our ancestors could deliver, in exchange for beads, mirrors, guns, gun-powder, shot, pots, pans, knives and axes.

Our ancestors, knowing a good bargain, set to work at once. Never had they been so busy. They went into the woods in the fall and emerged in the spring with cargoes of beaver pelts on their toboggans. Shipload after shipload of beaver pelts went to Europe. Our ancestors couldn't keep up with the demand.

The manufacturers of hats got rich. The kings and queens, emperors and empresses who owned the ships (HMS = His/Her Majesty's Ship) grew even richer. The Indians didn't get richer; they just succeeded in looking better.

As is bound to happen when men overkill or clear cut, sooner or later there will be little or nothing left to kill or cut, the goose lays fewer and fewer golden eggs. There were fewer and fewer shipments of beaver pelts, the shortage was felt all the way down the line. The hatters laid off employees, haberdasheries closed. Ships rode anchor, idle. Crews drank ale in public houses to pass the time. The Queen, as the principal owner of the fleet of idle ships, was royally pissed off. She demanded an explanation for the decline in business. But there were no economists to tell her exactly what caused the drop in production.

There were hints that it was the Indians' fault.

Her Highness sent for the chiefs of the Indian nations to account for their slowdown of production.

In Buckingham Palace the chiefs, arrayed in their finest headdresses and beaded jackets, their faces painted in the most artistic make-up, stood in the royal presence. Her Highness sat stiff necked to keep the royal crown in place. In her left hand she held the royal mace.

'My dear subjects,' the Queen droned. 'I am not amused by your dallying efforts in recent years. In former times you more than met your obligations, and even surpassed goals. What's wrong, Indians? Has success gone to your heads? Are you now too well off to work? Are you becoming lazy, … unreliable?' and Her Highness cast a withering stare at the assembled chiefs.

One of the chiefs stepped forward. 'All gone Quinn! All gone!' he apologized, turning the palms of his hands outward to show they were empty.

'What's all gone?'

'The beavers, Quinn!'

And that's the origin of Algonquin" Joe told me.

I have yet to hear a better explanation for ALGONQUIN.

My dear brothers, sisters, kin, aboriginals, and indigines (two more real beauts), don't be too upset by what these Latter Day Arrivals call us. Rather, if you don't know your language and your heritage, learn it and you will or should get to know who you are.

THINK INDIAN

KITCHI-MANITOU HAS GIVEN US A DIFFERENT UNDERSTANDING

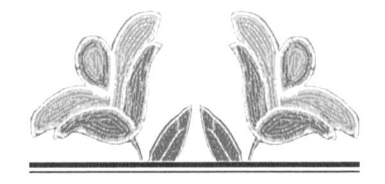

BASIL H. JOHNSTON, O.ONT., LLD., B.A. © 1998

Kitchi-Manitou Has Given Us

A Different Understanding

That there is a new interest in religions other than the traditional West European of Judaeo-Christian origin indicates that there is a growing recognition that other religions may have merit and validity, and that religion may have wider meaning and application than has heretofore been admitted.

Without belabouring the point, I submit that religion may either be formal or informal. A religion of the former order may be well structured, governed by a code of regulations and a hierarchy of clergy, governed by codes of laws and ethics and sanctions, administering its services through ceremonies and rituals performed in churches and temples. A religion of the latter kind may have no churches or priesthood, but it will have, though few and simple, rituals and ceremonies. Furthermore, it will possess an uncoded body of ethics. Though simple, a religion it still is.

Whether well organized and easily discernible, or loosely organized and hardly visible, what is important in religion is the essence and substance of its beliefs and understandings, and the mode of living out the beliefs.

If Indian religion is to be understood it must not be examined or regarded in terms of its structure or form, but rather in the essence and substance of the beliefs and understandings of the Natives that form the basis of some of the rituals and ceremonies.

But while neither the real substance nor the real merit of religion resides in ceremonies or rituals but in the daily living out of beliefs by people, nevertheless it is to ceremony that we turn for understanding. We do so because ceremony embodies in symbolic form men's understandings, views and attitudes toward life and matters relating to life.

There are numerous and striking Indian ceremonies: the Sun Dance, the Condolence Ceremony, the Feast of the Dead, the Snake Dance, which incorporate and image Indian beliefs in God, life, man and the world that could provide this understanding. Because it is no less replete in meaning than are the other great and striking ceremonies, and because I am a little more familiar with it than I am with the others, I have chosen the Pipe of Peace Smoking Ceremony.

Considered in its totality, the smoking was both a petition and a thanksgiving to the Creator; in another sense it represented man's relationships to his Maker, his fellow man, and to his world.

Considered in each of the acts that compose the entire ceremony, the smoke was a declaration of beliefs and understandings respecting life, death and living.

The substance used, tobacco, was the symbolic offering, an incense and a sacrifice, all at the same time. In the application of fire to the leaf was a tangible demonstration and evidence of creation and destruction, life and death, and the change of form of all substances.

Each act in the smoking reflected some belief about some aspect of life, living, and being.

By the first act, the offering of a whiff of vapour toward the sun, did the Anishinaubaek posit the being of the Master of Life, Kitchi-Manitou. While the smoke was breathed to the sun, the offering was in fact tendered to Kitchi-Manitou through the sun. In this mode, the Anishinaubaek acknowledged that all being and all life has its origin in and ultimately comes from Kitchi-Manitou, and that the sun is the physical agency through which the Master of Life confers his goodness and generosity.

In offering the whiff to the sun the Anishinaubaek were, by implication, affirming the spirituality and mystery of Kitchi-Manitou. In yet another way they were acknowledging that the Great Unknown could be known through his creations.

What was created was not so much an act of power, though it was that to be sure, but rather an act of generosity. And each act of generosity had to be acknowledged in some tangible way; hence the breath of smoke.

The second whiff of incense was to the earth. According to legend and tradition, ceremonies began with the creation of water, fire, stone and wind. It was from these substances that the physical world of sun, moon, earth and stars were formed. After earth were made plants, and then the animals; last, man. To all creatures earth was Mother. The offering of incense to the earth was an act of homage not only to the earth but to womanhood itself. For in the function of the earth was seen the gift of being and life, the fulfillment of purpose. The earth was woman; woman, earth. Both gave birth and life, both sustain being, growth and life, both enhance living; finally, both are primal.

But neither earth nor woman confers life alone. A woman, by special act with man, conceives and gives birth; the earth, by mystic union with the sun, through rain and heat generates beings and sustains life.

In tendering a whisper of incense to the earth, it is not only motherhood that is honoured; it is life-giving that is honoured, the wonderful miracle that is shared by woman and man, and permitted by Kitchi-Manitou.

As you honour your father and mother, so ought also you honour the sun and the earth.

And just as the first two breaths of smoke were offered in acknowledgement of the origin of life, and represented the attitude of men and women toward their creator and parents, so the next four whiffs blown toward the four cardinal directions that encompassed the world reflect the belief about the quality and tone of life and living, and the relationships to all orders of being and life.

After blowing smoke to the earth at his feet, the smoker turned to the east and blew a stream of vapour to that point on the horizon where the sun each day rose to bring a new dawning to all beings. To the Anishinaubaek each new rising was tantamount to a new life, a time new and different from that of the previous day. The previous day died with the sinking of the sun. Out of darkness rose the sun each day.

With the days there was a daily death and a daily birth, dissolution and regeneration.

At dawn the flowers opened, birds began to sing, men and women rose up refreshed, strong and ready for a new life. There was a miracle. For men and women and beasts there was an awakening from sleep, known as half death; for the world from the bond of night. Each morning represented a new start on life, a new life to live. Men, on rising from their pallets, unburdened by weariness and sorrow, went out of the lodge with hope in their hearts to face the east and intone a prayer of thanks.

The miracle that occurred in the physical order also occurred in the human order. The birth of a child is not much different from the coming of the dawn for the joy and hope it brings. Like the new day, the child has a life to live and purpose to fulfill. Like a new day that replaces the past, the infant will take the place of his parents and carry on the life. They are the links between the present and the future. For the children, men and women must labour. Because in the children will the spirit of the people continue to reside, and through life be transmitted and enlarged in succeeding generations.

The young, for their part, must grow and fulfill the wonderful promise of their birth and youth, otherwise the promise and youth is a nullity.

But birth and infancy is but one stage in the course of life. For a full and complete existence and living, three other stages, youth, adulthood and old age, must be traversed. During their progression through the stages a man or woman must fulfill themselves so that in the later phases of life they will have something to offer to their fellow men and to their community.

Then a breath of incense to the west, to that point on the compass where each day the sun sinks and loses its light. And with the waning of light the flowers enfold themselves, the birds cease their singing, and men and animals yield to half death, sleep.

Similarly in the human or moral orders men live out their lives, grow weak into decrepitude, and then expire. When man dies he is said to have taken a journey to the west to disappear like the sun over the rim of the world.

At death the body of the deceased is placed upon a platform with his feet toward the west and the body left exposed so as to enable the soul-spirit to leave its corporeal frame.

Man is a composite being made up of a corporeal substance which is finite, and an incorporeal substance which is capable of growth and is immortal. And it is this incorporeal substance that needs growth in all its aspects during its mortal existence, and that growth ought to have as its end and purpose accord, union between heart and mind for inner peace. There must be union of all parts of the inner being as there is a union, paradoxical as it may seem, between two contrary substances.

There is upon man and woman alike an obligation to develop the incorporeal substance or soul-spirit. At the same time the obligation is a challenge for, though the soul-spirit appears to be one and indivisible, it operates under different aspects. And so a man or a woman must try to know himself and understand his inner being. And because every man and every woman is endowed with differing powers and gifts of understanding, the individual alone and no other was deemed capable of understanding himself and, more especially, directing the growth of his inner self. A man was left alone in matters concerning his understanding and his exercise of the power of growth. He alone was answerable for his self-development.

And when a person had lived out his term of life upon earth, measured by the good performed or by length of life through to old age, he may enter the Land of Souls fulfilled and in peace.

Were a person to die before his term of life allotted to him expired, or he died unfulfilled or in inner turmoil, he would not find acceptance in the Land of Souls. According to some accounts the troubled soul might find rejection, and must return to earth to seek to infuse another being in the physical world or exist in exile outside the community of the Land of Souls.

From the west the principal smoker turned and offered a breath to the north, the origin of winter and the source of life perilous, and symbol of the way difficult. For the people of the north, who had annually to face and endure the ravages of winter, life was an ordeal. In the moral sense, life was regarded as consisting of four hills that had to be ascended and overcome, in the physical sense, as an ordeal.

To face the hardships of the ever changing climate, men had to develop courage, fortitude, endurance, patience and resourcefulness and cheerfulness. But more than that,

there was need to understand the laws that governed nature, and so regulate their lives according to the changes of the seasons and according as they saw the great physical laws.

In considering the laws that governed the physical world, the Anishinaubaek posited primal laws that regulated the movement of cosmic bodies, the coming and going of the seasons, the wax and wane of light and darkness, the division between water and fire, wind and rock. All other laws were predicated upon and were subsidiary to the first law.

The events of the world and the sequence of circumstances followed an order that was based upon the primary laws. There was harmony between the operation of the secondary laws and the primary. Birth was followed by growth, and growth was succeeded by decay; decay ended in death. Such was the natural sequence for all beings.

Men were dependent for their well-being upon the harmonious operations of laws, primary and secondary, and upon cosmic bodies remaining within their proper spheres. And though the seasons and the days and nights tended toward balance, there were times when the winters were too long, the days too cold. When excessive variations occurred, birth and growth and maturity were, in the plant and animal worlds, delayed and hindered. Over such changes man had no control; he had to live and labour and adjust to the changes.

Life was an ordeal. For leaders the whiff of smoke to the north was a reminder that decisions made in their councils were to be based upon the principle that "the well being of people took precedence over all other matters." What they were to avoid was making conditions and matters worse for their families and community, and during the smoking the leaders petitioned Kitchi-Manitou for wisdom. With wisdom, decisions could be reached that were just.

Life was an ordeal not only in the physical sense, but in a moral sense as well. Central to much of Indian life was the vision. The first portion of life, infancy and youth, was a period of preparation and quest for the vision. Both were arduous and difficult. The body had to be prepared and the soul-spirit had to be made ready. Only when both were rendered worthy by frequent testing did the vision come. After the vision, in the adult and old age stages, came the period of understanding and living out the vision. Perhaps the ordeal in the moral order was more demanding than that in the physical order.

Ordeal though the preparation and quest for the vision might have been; ordeal though accepting and living out the vision sometimes was, it was the event that wrought profound changes in a man's life. For prior to the vision, life was existence, preparation, receiving; after the vision, life became living, preparation became fidelity to the vision, receiving became giving. All acts thereafter took on a moral quality.

The last whiff of smoke was drawn and sent to the south. It was the act that embodied thanksgiving for all temporal gifts and good. The south imaged summer, birth, growth and fulfillment, green, yellow and brown. With the coming of spring and summer ended the hardship of winter. Men looked forward to the growth of food, the song of bird, the return of game, and the end of restriction, and a new beginning in freedom.

Men rejoice in witnessing in the cycle of time in the physical world the mystery of re-birth, the miracle of new life and growth. For it is only by seeing in the physical order birth and death, beginning and end, can life be understood and appreciated. For man, whose life and time is linear, there is no such certainty of re-birth in the physical order. There is but one end at death, a passage to and perhaps admission into the Land of Souls wherein there is a new and different existence, where even the essence of his soul-spirit changes. That is where the ordeal of life terminates and a new summer of existence begins.

Indian religion may have been without structure, without churches, without written codes, without clergy. It may have had few and simple ceremonies. But it was not without understandings and profound notions respecting life and man's place in the world order or man's nature.

This is not to say that eventually Indian religion might have become well and formally structured and organized. This is doubtful considering the inviolability of the individual's prerogative to inquire into himself and to foster his own inner growth according to his capacities.

In outlining Indian beliefs as they are symbolically embodied in the Pipe of Peace Smoking Ceremony, I must advert to the thesis "What is important in religion is the essence and substance of its beliefs and understandings, and the mode of living them out."

In this presentation I have sketched only the beliefs and views as I understand them. That is only part of religion. There is another portion, perhaps a more important portion; living out the beliefs that must not be separated from the beliefs.

THINK INDIAN

Considering only the beliefs and insights is tantamount to the incomplete axiom "seek the truth." For religion to have meaning it must be lived out. For "seek the truth" to have meaning a man must be true.

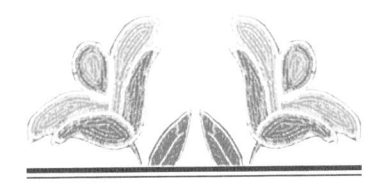

THINK INDIAN

BASIL H. JOHNSTON, O.ONT., LLD., B.A. © 1998

Think Indian

"Think Indian" bumper stickers pleaded and advocated in the 60's, "Think Indian."

And while the plea may have been intended for general consideration, it represented in many instances a personal appeal for the exercise of a greater degree or intensity of Indianness, particularly by those who were prevented, for a variety of reasons, from practicing real Indianness.

Youth who lived in cities and youth who did not speak the tribal language most keenly felt this incompleteness of spirit and being. To gain the fullness of their heritage, some went the rounds of pow-wows; others took to drumming.

How youth felt, and how some youth sought to acquire this sense of completeness may not be better exemplified than by the following story.

Both his parents were Anishinaubae. In colour and in feature he was Anishinaubae. With such heritage and traits one could hardly be more Anishinaubae than that. Yet the young man did not feel fully Anishinaubae.

Like many others, he sought this completeness in books and by attending conferences; he wrote articles and delivered talks; he wore beads, and ate wild rice, danced at pow-wows and smoked the sacred pipe. But none of these exercises instilled in him a sense of fulfillment; rather, they only served to reinforce his feeling of want in his being.

Something was missing, but the young man was unable to establish what it was that subtracted from his sense of wholeness. The old people at home had this constituent, whatever it was; the old men and women whom he met at pow-wows were endowed with it. And he envied them their assurance and their dignity.

At pow-wows and at ball tournaments the youth deliberately sought the companionship of the elders, for they had what he did not; and he believed that by association with the old men and the old women he would find what he was looking for. But they did not take him in as readily as he had hoped. On almost every occasion they would eventually revert to Anishinaubae, their tribal language, … his language. At that moment the young man was outcast; he was not fully one of them. Without language, he could not share in the tribal soul or its spirit, or in its laughter or its sorrows. Though he was a member of the tribe, he did not fully belong.

Only language, the young man decided, would confer upon him a wholeness that would quench the hunger of his spirit. But that would take years, perhaps too long. He wanted to be Indian, Anishinaubae not only in appearance but in outlook and in attitude as well, now, soon, and who better to instruct him in the beliefs and understandings of the tribe than a medicine man.

However, not just any medicine man would do; only the most respected. Eventually the youth learned of such a man, and he wrote him a letter asking for an appointment.

On the day of the appointment the young man offered tobacco to the medicine man as prescribed by custom. The youth then explained the purpose of his visit, and told the medicine man that he had come for guidance and instruction in attaining peace of spirit.

To "would you teach me?" all the medicine man said was "Keen igoh" (It's up to you).

Because "keen igoh" was delivered in an off-handed manner and tone, the young man interpreted it as a question of his sincerity, and assured the old man that he had not made the long trip for nothing, and that he would arrive on the 15th of June and remain till the end of August. Not only would he pay room and board and whatever fee the medicine man might assess, but the young man volunteered to perform whatever chores his tutor and his wife might assign. "I'm not coming up for nothing."

"I'll be waiting for you, then," the medicine man said.

On the 15th of June the young man arrived at the medicine man's home, anxious to begin his lessons in Indian-Anishinaubae culture.

After breakfast the following day the medicine man took his apprentice, for that is how the young man regarded himself, into the forest. Nothing could have been more fitting on that occasion for the young man than to learn about one's self and about life than in the habitat most natural to that of his tribe. Did not his ancestors derive their knowledge from birds, animals, plants and trees? And the young man marvelled how it was possible for anyone to learn from woodpeckers, porcupines, frogs and such creatures about the properties of plants.

All morning they walked, the young man following close upon the heels of the medicine man, eager to hear some remark or comment, but the old man said not a word, nor did he point to any plant, as the young man fully expected, to refer to its name or to describe its uses. Not even during lunch did the medicine man offer to explain anything or provide words of wisdom; instead he prattled on about the weather and what it was likely to do to the crops of blueberries and other plants. Nor was the afternoon any different from that of the morning; it was walk, walk, walk, without a word passing between them.

The young man found silence hard to bear; it was because he was unaccustomed to it and he fully expected discussion. The silence he could bear, but almost unendurable were the blackflies, mosquitoes, deer flies and other nits and gnats. But the young man set his jaw in determination and slapped at flies and scratched until he bled. He maintained his own silence.

It was not until they were about to go to bed that the medicine man made any kind of reference to the day's session. He asked, "Well! Did you see anything?"

The young man had to think if he had seen anything unusual and worth remembering, but he could recall nothing. He shook his head and said "no."

"Did you hear anything?"

Except for birds, whose calls he could not distinguish, and for squirrels and mosquitoes, the young man had heard nothing worth mentioning. "No" he said, shaking his head at the same time.

As he lay in the dark, the young man pondered these questions. "What did you see? What did you hear?" To him they were peculiar questions, not at all relevant to his needs and purposes; certainly they were not the kind of questions that prompted intellectual inquiry. What did they mean? Whatever the worth or purpose of the questions, the young man resolved to be more observant. One never knew what the old man may have had in mind.

After one week the young man was growing weary of the same daily routine, answering the same questions, "Did you see anything? Did you hear anything?" Perhaps he might have to tolerated the routine and the nits and gnats had he been learning something, but he was no better informed then than he had been when he arrived. At the same time the young man began to doubt that the medicine man could teach. In his misgivings he made up his mind that if the medicine man taught him nothing over the next week, he would go home.

Next day they took another direction. At least this constituted a change in the routine, though in all other respects it was identical.

Around mid-morning the old man stopped by a pool of water. At its edge he sat on his haunches and gazed into the bottom. The young man too, in imitation of the medicine man, sat on his haunches, and he too gazed into the water, but he could not see what object so absorbed his tutor. There was nothing in the bottom of the pool except twigs, old leaves, branches, pebbles and little creatures; on the surface, water bugs. There was nothing there, yet the medicine man was looking into the water as if there was something there. Curious as he was to know what the old man beheld, still the young man declined to ask, "What are you looking at?" to avoid being regarded as too forward or as inobservant.

But the question burned on in the young man's mind all afternoon. It was not until evening that he had an opportunity of bringing the matter up, as casually as he could manage, during their conversation.

"I've been trying to decide what it was that you were looking at in the pool this morning."

"I was looking at myself," the old man replied deliberately, while fixing his gaze upon the young man. "And what were looking at?" he added.

"I wasn't looking at anything in particular; I was too busy trying to spot what you were looking at."

"Then, you didn't see yourself?"

The young man, not knowing quite what to make of the medicine man's remark, hesitated for a moment before he replied, "I guess not."

As he lay in bed that night the young man could not decide whether his tutor was serious or trifling with him about looking at himself in the water. What good would that do? What would he learn? How would that instill in him an Indianness? Decent as he was, the old man's habits and his questions did not quite conform to the young man's notions as to how a medicine man ought to deport himself and how to instruct. Before another day was dissipated in pointless trekking through the bush with no knowledge gained, the young man decided that he would have to ask for instructions directly.

It was as if he had known the young man's thoughts; the first thing that the old man said at breakfast was, "Today I'll teach you some medicine. Take you to pick roots."

At last. The day that the young man had long awaited. At last he would learn something.

They drove over old bush roads and then walked an old trail tangled with growth before they at last came to a marsh. Beneath their boots water oozed from the spongy ground. The air was rank with the brackish odour of the waters of the marsh. Yet, floating on the glasslike surface were water lilies, white and yellow, numerous beyond counting; like blossoms they bloomed.

While the young man reflected on the co-existence of beauty and ugliness as he regarded the swamp, and defended himself from the nits and gnats, the medicine man studied the water lilies as if he were taking stock of their qualities.

"Get me that flower over there," the medicine man said at length, pointing to a plant some distance from where they stood. According to the young man's calculation the medicine man was pointing to a plant in the middle of the pond.

Wishing to please, the young man sat down to take off not only his shoes but his trousers as well, but the medicine man bade him keep his clothing on to protect his feet from sharp objects and from leeches. He would have gone himself, but since the young man was anxious to learn and needed experience, the medicine man said that he would give the young man some practice in harvesting medicinal roots.

It was not without misgivings that the youth stepped fully clothed into the stagnant murky waters. He made his way forward tentatively, feeling his way with his feet and closing his hand around the stalks of reeds and water lilies to keep his balance, as an old infirm man or a child might dodder.

When the water was waist high, the young man turned and pointed at a water lily nearest him, shouting, "This one?"

"No! Farther out."

The young man waded further out, stopping only when he stood chest deep in the water. Once more he shouted, "This one?"

"No! That one over there."

Still further he went, until he stood near the middle, with only his head protruding. "This one?"

"Yeah."

The young man was about to break off the flower from the stem.

"No! No! No! The whole of the plant, roots and all," the old man shouted in alarm.

The young man was already nauseated by the stench of the stagnant waters, or so he considered them, and he was revolted by the slime of the weeds and the slick of leeches; now he was repelled by the very thought of immersing himself in the dank waters.

Despite his qualms and queasiness, the young man nevertheless drew himself under by means of the stalk of the water lily. Underwater, he traced the roots. Within seconds he surfaced, sputtering and gasping for breath. From then on, until the plant was extracted in its entirety, it was a series of divings and surfacings.

And that is how the young man reaped medicine all that day, but he did not remain with the medicine man; the next day he packed his belongings and returned to his home in southern Ontario.

It was not until some years later that the youth, while looking at the snow swirling outside his window and thinking about his experience with the medicine man, that he finally saw what it was that the old man was trying to impart. To the young man it was like revelation. From that moment the youth understood what he had to do to be Indian, to "Think Indian."

What do the words "Think Indian" mean? What is it that has inspired the words "Think Indian?" What is it that the words advocate? For whom are they intended?

It is not a mode of thought or unique manner of perception indigenous to the original Native peoples of this continent that was being advocated; rather, it seemed that it was a plea to all Native people not to neglect their heritage; it was a reminder to all that there was something worthwhile in the heritage deserving of perpetuation in new and different modes and forms; it was a petition to anyone who would care to listen, to continue to commemorate the ceremonies and to abide by the principles that gave direction to our ancestors.

There was a time when the original peoples of this continent needed no reminder to "Think Indian" or "Be Indian." They were. In those days the Anishinaubaek, Six Nations, Athabaskan, Inuit, the Souian, Salishan, Cree, Blackfoot, Micmac, Haidan and other tribes were in possession of and had tenure upon the entire breadth and depth of the land and the waters. All that they were came from the land and the sea. They drew their sustenance and strength from it; they derived their sense of direction and their place in the order of nature from it; they sought their visions and gave them meaning in their lives; they invoked Kitchi-manitou and performed their ceremonies upon Mother Earth; and through the exercise of their potential upon the earth and sea, reaped their sense of worth and freedom. They were masters of their destinies.

But they lost their lands, together with almost every means by which they might yet find sustenance and strength, direction and place, visions and meanings, and to till their potential until it yielded independence of spirit and person. Without either the language or the means to find purpose and fulfillment, there was little opportunity for many Native brothers and sisters to foster an identity. Unable to find purpose or fulfillment within tribal sphere or without, their resolve of spirit waned. These, then, were the circumstances that gave rise to the present situation and occasioned the plea to "Think Indian" and to regain what had been lost.

How is "Think Indian" to be understood? How is it to be animated? How is it to be exercised in daily life?

It is not so much a mode of thought as it is an understanding of one's duties and fulfilling those duties. To "Think Indian" is to care about family and tribe, to look after the elderly and the poor and the weak and the children. A man was to feed his family and to risk his life for the well-being of his tribe. The same custom that established men's duties also prescribed that women tend the sick and the village, and to instruct the children so that tribal heritage passed on from generation to generation.

Such duties, few and simple as they were, exacted and required onerous personal demands and training. Think of the conditions then prevailing! Think of the weaponry! Think of the resources and equipment. Hunters, and sometimes their families, had to walk miles and days in search of game. All that a hunter had was a bow and arrow of limited range; a fisherman a fragile spear. All nature allowed the hunter or the fisherman was one chance. Merely to draw close enough to game to fire an arrow or deliver one thrust with spear demanded all the skill, patience, discipline, fortitude and strength that only years of experience and training could confer upon a man.

And there was no exemption from these duties. Every young man, regardless of talent or disposition or stature or vitality, either yielded to or freely accepted the discipline and training necessary for the development of his potential that enabled him to carry out his duties. At stake was his survival, the well-being of his family, and the safety of his tribe. There was little margin for error or carelessness; none for indolence.

With so much at stake it is little wonder, then, that the tribe demanded and expected much of its members. Youth was challenged and tested in marksmanship, for strength in wrestling, for endurance in racing, for fortitude in fasting, for resourcefulness in play and pantomime, patience in stalking small game, and daring in lone vigil in preparation for the rigours along the Path of Life. In serving the tribe, there were no rewards.

To submit to discipline and to endure whatever hardships that may occur in the performance of duties or in the course of work in the service of the tribe was to "Think Indian."

THINK INDIAN

There was also another way in which "Think Indian" found expression and exercise in previous generations. The Native people, then, admired certain qualities above that of others, believing that such qualities endowed men and women with a greater degree of humanity and conferred a dignity upon the tribe. Even more honoured than was courage, resourcefulness, fortitude and other traits was generosity. The tribe fostered generosity in two ways. On the one hand, it condemned selfishness as the worst aspect of human nature and, on the other hand, lauded selflessness. In some tribes the formal renunciation of selfishness during ceremony was essential for admission into society. Generosity, more than any other quality or means, fostered brotherhood and sisterhood.

The hunter, the fisherman, the medicine woman, were honoured and respected as much for the act and spirit that they represented as much as the exercise of skill. For the hunter, the fisherman and the medicine woman, the act of giving was, in effect, a sharing of the bounty of Mother Earth with those equally entitled to the yield. No finer tribute could

have been paid to anyone than to have said of them, "He is a kind man," "She is a kind woman," for offering to the widow food, to the stranger shelter, and to the unwell medicine and care.

When a man seeks a dream or a woman incenses herself with sweetgrass, they are either expressing a belief or enacting one in ritual. Understanding and ritual are to "Think Indian." In The Sun Dance, The Hah-Mah-Tsa, The Pipe of Peace, and The Feast of the Dead and other great public ceremonies are embodied what the Natives of whatever tribe understood of Kitchi-manitou, life, death, good and evil. To take part in these ceremonies was to affirm the understandings of the tribe. There was almost, among all, a reverence for the mystery of life, Manitou, not only as it animated humankind, but also as it vitalized animal-kind and plant-kind, and the earth itself. The hunter and the fisherman besought the pardon of the manitous, mysteries, who presided over the animals of the forest and of the beings of the sea; women who prepared the plants for healing invoked the manitous to impress their curative powers upon the herbs. To hold that the bear and the buffalo, the whale and the salmon, the partridge and the ptarmigan were as entitled to life as humankind, and to render them that due in thought as well as in spirit was to "Think Indian," and not merely lip service.

But it is not enough to "Think Indian;" it is not enough to say "this I believe;" it is not enough to wear ornaments. More is required. The ideas must be sought, and the understandings must be fulfilled. Only then will "Think Indian," combined with fulfillment, have meaning. Through accomplishment, the plea or advocation "Think Indian" will transform into "Be Indian."

How, then, is "Think Indian" to be given expression and meaning today, now that the trails, and the sea, and the plains and the forest no longer provide arenas for tests or occasions to foster a sense of worth? How is "Think Indian" to be nurtured now that only a few undertake a quest for vision for revelation and inspiration? How is "Think Indian" to be restored in an age when even human life has lost a great deal of meaning? How is "Think Indian" to comfort abandoned and neglected children? How is "Think Indian" to be instilled in youth who do not understand the language? How is "Think Indian" to heal the spirit ravaged by drugs and alcohol? How? How?

Even though men no longer hunt with bow and arrow or spear, or women cook with heated stones, and the mode of life is so different from what it once used to be, the conditions now prevailing have not altered the need for demand upon self. Indeed, the need may even be greater. Only the form and the sphere of testing have changed. No longer does youth track a deer for hours, or risk life amidst a herd of buffalo, or wait in the Arctic cold for a seal, or mourn for a year for a departed loved one. Now a youth may operate a lathe or draw diagrams or operate a computer or listen to a stethoscope. And the sphere of testing is now the classroom and the office. Whether the school or the office building are the best arenas for testing or demonstrating proof of worth is questionable, but these are the spheres in which Native people must excel.

As the tribe, through its elders, made demands upon youth, so must teachers today make demands upon youth. The parents too must make demands, as once their ancestors made demands and expected much from their children. It ought to be no different today from what it was in times gone by when men and women subjected their sons and daughters to the same rigours on the trail and in the camp that they themselves endured. To expect less in the classroom or in the study-hall is to do a disservice not only to the child but to the tribe as well. To make demands upon and to encourage youth to make demands upon themselves is to "Think Indian."

And what of youth? Is the need for demand of self and demonstration of worth less today than formerly? Has the need for Quest of Vision diminished in this computer age? Is the need for service to tribe diminished by the availability of consultants? Are tribal understandings and tribal heritage now to be merely studied as minerals, land forms, and historical facts are studied, without application to daily life? What is youth to do?

Youth today must make demands upon itself as their predecessors in previous generations have done. It is said that conditions and circumstances are hard today; teachers are indifferent; textbooks are biased; fellow students are sometimes prejudiced; courses are irrelevant. Conditions a century or more in the past were no less difficult. Experience was the only teacher then, and vastly more intolerant; the forests, meadows, seas and ice which served as a book may not have been biased, but they exacted of everyone alike mastery of lessons; at times there was the risk of ambush or the sudden raid; to many the bow, the arrow, the spear, the flint were irrelevant; they made them relevant.

In previous generations, youths' destiny was to hunt and fish, plant and gather, heal and lead, make war, and honour the Manitous in serving the tribe. No longer, except for a few. Today's youth has greater scope. They may aspire for careers in medicine, physics, law, chemistry, accounting, astronomy, journalism, or any other profession that offers a challenge and makes demands upon talent and spirit. And to aspire to such careers does not render one less Micmac or Mohawk or Cree, any more than the acceptance of a musket or metal pot made the man and woman less Montagnais or less Ottawa. In fact, the youth accepting these demands imposed upon him or her in the attainment of these careers with the same degree of effort as the hunter and fisherman and the medicine woman of previous generations is exercising "Think Indian."

And perhaps it is with talents as doctors, engineers, lawyers, architects, entrepreneurs and physicists that youth may best serve their communities and peoples. The tribe's need is no less urgent today than it was in former times. While the tribe's needs were, in a sense, simple, today's issues go far beyond the fulfillment of basic needs; those issues bear upon rights and title to land and sovereignty and identity itself. For over 150 years, the tribes and their communities have been ill-served by a succession of agents, assistant agents, commissioners, community development workers and quasi-social workers in the administration of programs and policies. If today's youth is to emulate their ancestors in the exercise of selflessness in the discharge of their duties toward their kin, neighbours, children and grandchildren and their community, then youth ought to seek that training that best prepares them to serve their peoples.

And though it is difficult and impossible for youth and today's generation to live as their ancestors once lived, the Native people of today can do more, and must do more, than merely study culture in school or discuss them in the abstract. They must live out those ancient principles and make them part of their lives insofar as circumstances allow. To do so is to "Think Indian."

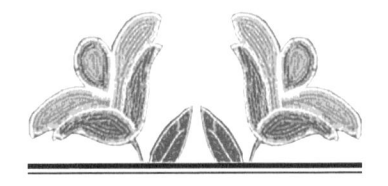

LOOKING BACK

FROM WRITING TO PUBLICATION

BASIL H. JOHNSTON, O.ONT., LLD., B.A. © 2000

Looking Back

From Writing to Publication

Around 1963 the country rediscovered Indians; Indians didn't know quite how to receive their rediscovery after scores of years of neglect. Actually, it was Kahn-Tineta Horn, a striking Mohawk fashion model from Kanawake, Quebec, who stirred Indians out of their lassitude and into joining her entourage. White male reporters, pens poised to record her utterances, tongues hanging out, trailed and tailed Miss Horn wherever she went.

Not to be outdone, Indian male leaders emerged. Canadian leaders, anxious to see justice done, joined the Indian cause and formed organizations such as the Indian-Eskimo Association, and organized conferences.

One of the first and one of the largest up to that time was the Glendon College Conference held in Toronto in 1968.

It's doubtful that there was as much hype about Indians as there was preceding the conference since the Cleveland Indians were in the World Series in 1948. Deputy Ministers, University Presidents, Rectors and a raft of academics were rumoured to be present. The American Indian Movement warriors were going to be in attendance. Last and least was a small contingent of no-name Indians who were to serve as seminar leaders. It was to be a memorable event.

On the morning of the commencement of the conference the atmosphere was fairly crackling. The questions that were burning in everyone's mind were, "How many warriors would invade the college? What would they do?" With the warriors' presence, something was bound to happen. And we, no-names, were going to be part of an historic event.

I stood at the back of the hall with Jim Turner and Vic Pelletier, friends now deceased. We too were excited. We stood on tip toe to look over the heads of the people standing in front. We whispered our guesses as to how many warriors would come stomping in, how they would be attired, how armed, what they would say, and what they would do. "Hope they tell it like it is," Vic growled, repeating the popular expression of the day.

THINK INDIAN

At 9:00 AM, the official platform filed in and occupied their places on the stage, grave White men, grim Indians. The Master of Ceremonies introduced the official and distinguished guests, reciting litanies of their accreditations and accomplishments. There were polite, subdued rounds of applause. Actually, no one was much interested in the army of anthros and sociologists. Who mattered now, from the Indian point of view, were the warriors.

Three prominent AIM leaders were to have been with the platform party, as stars of the conference, but had not arrived in time to take part in the grand entry. The conference couldn't start without them. Meanwhile the Master of Ceremonies made talk to keep the audience amused. His jokes went beneath the dignity and intelligence of the academic crowd. After several minutes of nervous waiting, there was a commotion to the left of the platform. All heads and eyes were fixed to the entrance!

"The warriors that we've been waiting for are here" the Master of Ceremonies announced. Three warriors, none over 5'5" or 140 lbs., red tams perched on their heads, fists raised aloft in defiance, marched onto the platform and made for the microphone.

The crowd cheered, stamped their feet, clapped their hands and yelled "Sock it to us! Sock it to us!" in imitation of Judy Carne, the "sock it to me" gal of Laugh In, the well known TV program.

"Sock it to us" the crowd demanded. Yes, they deserved to be socked. They felt guilty; they were guilty. But it was difficult to tell whether the crowd was really repentant and wished to make amends or were just shooting off their mouths for the benefit of the press. For the Indians in the audience there was ample reason to belt someone in the teeth; not just anyone but especially clergymen, priests, teachers, nuns, police, politicians and civil servants. Indians joined the clamour, yelling out lustily, "Sock it to them."

But instead of a call to arms, a sock it to them as we had expected, the AIM spokesman gave an apology for his less than warrior-like spirit. "Come a long ways, us, hardly got any sleep." Down went our collective expectations.

If the speaker had dared us, "Come! Let us march on the Indian Affairs Branch," I like to think in retrospect that we would have been foolhardy enough to march west on Lawrence Avenue, down Mount Pleasant Avenue as far as St. Clair Avenue, and then west. What the mob would have done with the Regional offices of the Indian Affairs Branch is anyone's guess.

After the bubble burst on the platform, the Master of Ceremonies reviewed the program for the long week-end and the day, then sent the seminar leaders and their registrants to their appointed rooms.

Not knowing much about seminars I asked my group what format they wished me to follow.

"Just tell us about your heritage" someone growled.

I was staggered by the tone of the voice and the enormity of fulfilling the speaker's demand. Where to start! I was ill prepared to tell about my heritage that would satisfy the audience and do justice to my background. I beat around the bush, hoping to convince the audience that I knew what I was saying. While I was beating around the woods, another member of my seminar pointed out to me, "You can't go back to the bow and arrow days. You can't even look back. Bear in mind what happened to Lot's wife when she took one backward glance.

The speaker's reminder was a stupid, thoughtless remark, prompted by an assumption that there is little or nothing in our heritage worth remembering or preserving.

Despite the fate of Lot's wife for looking back, it is nevertheless a useful thing to look back on occasion to see how far we've come, what we've accomplished, and to check our bearings to see that we are still on course. It was a useful thing for the prodigal son to look back and to return to his roots.

We as Anishinaubaek must look back, not to revive the bow and arrow or restore the war club or re-establish the wigwam, but to take up once more those ideals, values, principles, understandings and attitudes that made us what we are, and confer upon us a character and singularity that deserve to live on. We as writers must look back and look ahead if we are to fulfill our functions and discharge our obligations to our communities and to our people. We as writers must understand the past, for inspiration, edification, illumination, and for growth.

I have often been asked, "Is it difficult to publish?" The answer is "yes".

Let me outline first some of the difficulties and afterward indicate what your advantages may be as Anishinaubae peoples. First, publishers want imaginative, well written manuscripts that reflect fresh interpretations and viewpoints.

The craft of writing itself is one of the most difficult of the arts. It demands skill in the construction of sentences and paragraphs, precision in expression, imagination in the development of themes and ideas, industry in submitting to daily work until the task is complete. But if the writer does not have a broad life, a fine sense in distinguishing, discernment in fact and fancy, good judgement in assessing character, and a commitment to the highest degree of accuracy, he would be lacking in INTEGRITY.

I will not elaborate upon all the points that I have referred to. But I would like to make special mention of reading and practice in the development of your craft and art.

If you are to develop your range and scope, you must read, and read widely. You must read the masters: Dickens, Stevenson, McCauley, Huxley, Newman, Shakespeare, Milton, Arnold, Hugo, Voltaire, Rousseau, Addison, Steele, Shelley, Keats, Byron, Maugham, Plutarch, Carlisle, Dante, Scott, Burke, Momaday, Lewis, Conrad, Pater, Dawson, Belloc, Forester, Lamb, Hemingway, Proust, Austen, Plato, Aristotle, Livy, Horace, Virgil, Pliny,

Aristophanes, Sophocles, and other great writers. You must read and study the bible, history, law, economics, philosophy, logic, language; and listen to the stories of your people.

You can do no better, if you are to polish your craft, than take the advice of Professor Lounsbury who wrote, "The art of writing, like that of painting and sculpture, is an imitative art," and Robert L. Stevenson, one of the greatest stylists in the English language, who said, "Whenever I read a book or passage that particularly pleased me, in which a thing was said or an effect rendered with propriety, in which there was either some perspicuous force or some happy distinction in style, I must sit down at once and set myself to ape that quality. That, like it or not, is the way to learn to write; whether I have profited or not, that is the way." I recommend it to you.

And even if you were to write a manuscript that may merit publication, your chances are slim. Some publishing houses may receive anywhere between 100 and 125 unsolicited manuscripts each week. There are thousands of writers and would-be writers; competition is keen. A beginning writer does not and cannot expect his or her manuscript to be read immediately upon submission. It could take months. A smaller publisher may assess a manuscript much more quickly than a larger one. But in choosing a publisher, size and reputation are important considerations. A small firm may be more willing to publish your first effort, but it may not have the reputation or the resources or the marketing organization to promote your book. Whatever choice you make will have a bearing upon the degree of success your book may have. In my own case, having McClelland and Stewart and Key Porter as my publishers is a fortunate circumstance and reflects my approach that may be expressed by, "Go after the Big Boys and the Big Girls; nothing lost, much gained." Without disclosing in detail precisely what my approach was, I had my manuscript read and deemed good enough for publication within two weeks of submission. I was fortunate. With a little imagination and resourcefulness, you may overcome all sorts of delays and obstacles.

An author may wait months for some reply from a publisher. The answer may take the form of a rejection slip. Don't be discouraged. There are many authors of substance whose first manuscript was rejected many times before publication. I have heard that "Watership Down" was rejected at least eight times before it was finally published. Do not regard or accept as final one editor's opinion or pronouncement upon the merit of your manuscript.

Even after publication there is no assurance that your book will sell. It may sit on bookshelves unsold, unread. The public is the final judge, whether you like it or not, whether they can discern between what is good or bad. That is the way it is. Should your manuscript sooner or later be published, consider yourself lucky.

Apart from the preferences of editors who may deem your manuscript unsuitable for publication, there is the mass of manuscripts to contend with and the public taste to satisfy. Of this situation, Mordecai Richler, one of the country's finest writers, is reported to have said that owing to the quantity of trash written, it is harder to publish today than formerly. I agree with that assessment, but for a different reason. It is not the quality of writing that may ultimately be at fault but the taste of readers. Many will read tripe and trash. An author may labour to write well only to find his work rejected by many readers who prefer mediocrity.

And if competition and public taste make publication of worthwhile manuscripts more difficult, there is yet public sensitivity that increases the hardship. By public sensitivity I mean that which the public may or may not allow to be said or written about certain matters and groups of people. Precluded from publication by this norm is writing that is discriminatory and defamatory. A work may not find its way into print if it is deemed too right-wing or too left-wing. A manuscript ought to meet certain standards.

"And it is good that authors should be remunerated," Lord Babington-Macaulay advocated. The anticipation of royalties and gain, and the freedom that go with writing is one of the incentives that urge writers to slave at their desks. Make no mistake about that. But, unless you are a Harold Robbins, Arthur Hailey, Gore Vidal, or some proven renowned author, or have some lurid matter to reveal, there is no large advance against royalties to make you work and live in comfort while you are belabouring over your epic. You will have to wait for the royalties to trickle in, and the total in the end may not have justified your effort or attained your expectations. In the meantime, while you are awaiting a windfall, what then? Beginning authors are usually poor. There are several sources: the Canada Council, the Ontario Arts Council, foundations and patrons, if they can be found.

Some years ago when I began to write I was persuaded to apply to the Canada Council for a grant to enable me to write a great work; something new, something that had never before been attempted. I thought that the Canada Council would share in my excitement. Alas! My idea and enterprise was rejected on the ground that I was not sufficiently academically qualified. It was not the work that was turned down; it was my qualifications that were dismissed. What hurt was that in the same year, an applicant with the appropriate degrees was granted a sum of money to enable him to research and publish a paper comforting to Communism while at the same time detracting to this nation.

Since being rejected for a grant 30 years earlier, I had been in an unroyal snit. Three years ago I decided to suspend my snit and apply for a Canada Council grant from its Aboriginal Section. With 13 books to my credit, the Council and its Aboriginal Section would fling money my way. But instead of doing that, the Council flung another rejection in my face. There were 80 other better manuscripts, the Aboriginal Section Head wrote.

It is not easy to get grants. Yet I know of no other way for beginning authors, and even some established authors, to sustain themselves while they are writing.

Should an author be so lucky as to get a commitment from a publisher to publish his work, he ought immediately to secure the services and counsel of a lawyer; not just any lawyer but one who specializes in copyright. The beginning author should never attempt to negotiate contracts or legal matters, for a couple of reasons. In the first place, covenants are difficult and are usually beyond the grasp of the lay person; and second, negotiations can become bitter and impair the author-editor relationship. Moreover, it is sound business practice to have legal counsel represent the author. Besides being an art, writing is a business, and should be regarded and conducted as such.

It is only fair that after having outlined some of the difficulties in getting published, to offer a brief sketch of what I regard as advantages for you and me, Indian authors. And my remarks are based on the belief that publishers want something new, something fresh; a new and novel interpretation to old themes and, of course, sound writing.

Over the years, but especially during the past few years that I have been writing, I have turned more and more to the legends, myths, stories, ceremonies, songs and language of my people. What a wealth of themes, insights, approaches, understandings of life, human nature and character, and all aspects and phases of human endeavour that there is, still untouched. What a treasure there is for you and me to write plays, stories, satire, poems, humour, novels, essays. What a storehouse of ideas, concepts, new and different, that may add to the general understanding of life and man. What an opportunity for you and me to explore and discover what is in our heritage. What advantages you have as one of the first in relatively new horizons, in writing and offering to others some observation, knowledge, wisdom, insight, that is different. The scope is unlimited. It is in the old legends, myths and stories that I have found my inspiration and direction. It is by looking back that I have come to understand our people better and appreciate our heritage more clearly.

You must look back. You and I must seek in our past, not reason for identity, not causes for anger and resentment, though there is that to be sure, but for breadth and scope and depth to sustain your work and to keep your fund of ideas ever abundant. You and I must ever look back to make sure that what we do and say today reflects truly what we may impart; you and I must look to the past for guidance in our thoughts and interpretations; you and I must look to the past with gratitude for bestowing upon us an abundance of ideas for our talents. It is for you and me to take the legacy conferred upon us by the past, give it new and fresh expression in the present, and if our talents permit, for the benefit of the future.

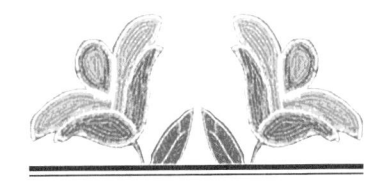

Tom Didn't Fail!

He Succeeded

Basil H. Johnston, O.Ont., LLD., B.A. © 2000

Tom Didn't Fail!

He Succeeded

Tom, as he told me, was like many other boys who had ascended to the dizzy heights of grade 8. He was one of the big boys now, in his last year of public school. The year following he would be even more exalted, walking in the hallways of a high school.

School was a drag, teachers were walking bores, study was for wimps and sissies, not for macho young men. Besides, passing was a breeze. He'd already breezed into grade 8. He'd breeze out as easily as he had breezed into it.

Macho was what he was going to be, like some of his friends as they wanted him to be. It was macho to slouch in class. It was groovy to make smart-assed remarks in class that got the teacher's dander up and drew sniggers from his friends. It was cool to swagger around the school yard and in the classroom. He got the attention that he wanted from his teacher and from the other students.

After school Tom and his friends dawdled on the road smoking cigarettes like miniature Marlboro men, telling smutty jokes and using four-letter words, goofing off to attract the attention of girls.

Evenings after supper, and assuring his parents that he had little or no homework, Tom went out again with his friends to prowl the roads or to hang out at the local store. There they'd drool as their concupiscences were aroused by the sight of girls. They looked up to young men who strutted to and from the store, wishing to be like this one or that one who wasn't "scared of nothin', him!"

June and the examinations were ages away. There were bundles of time.

In the meantime Tom's mother nagged, "Get your homework done! Why don't you stay home for once? Your brothers didn't waste their time as you are doing. You've got to work to succeed."

And so the months slipped by and away; June sneaked in almost unnoticed.

Examinations were three weeks off. What a drag having to stay in evenings to read about Hamilton's steel industry, read bleeding poetry. Tom was a tad nervous. As long as he got 50%, he'd pass. He'd always got by in the past. The thought gave him some comfort.

Tom struggled in and through the examinations. Questions were hard, harder than what he'd expected. Teacher asked questions that weren't in the text. Just like the teacher to ask trick, unexpected questions. Despite his difficulties, Tom still thought that he'd done OK! At least he tried to convince himself that he'd written a decent paper. Still he was worried, a state of mind that he'd never before experienced.

"How'd you do?" his parents asked.

"I did OK," Tom assured them.

"Well, you should! Your brothers passed with honours."

On the last day of school Tom took his report card from his teacher, who wished him "Better luck next time!"

It was an odd remark that didn't bode well.

Before leaving school, Tom slipped into the washroom where he opened the unsealed envelope. 41%! His heart beat faster, his knees shook. He read the teacher's comment, "Tom has the ability to excel. But the trouble with Tom is that he doesn't have the drive to match his ability. He's destined for mediocrity."

DESTINED FOR MEDIOCRITY! Tom felt like running away. What would his parents say?

At home he put "the report" on the table, then retreated into his room, there to await the call to sentence. Tom shivered.

Around 5:30 PM his mother came home. Tom could hear her rummaging now here, now there.

"TOM!" the voice was sharp. "TOM! GET OUT HERE! AT ONCE!"

Tom crept out.

"What's this mean? FAILED! Didn't I tell you to study....You're a disgrace to the family ... a poor example of this community!" and his mother heaped damnation and exasperation upon Tom's sloth. "We didn't raise you up to be a failure!" The door's opening interrupted her tirade, for a moment. She resumed, "Look at this! Your brother's failed!"

"Tom failed?" his brothers looking at him chorused. "How could you, Tom?" they asked in unison.

Tom had no answer.

The tirade resumed, and continued until their father came home an hour later.

"Look at this!" Tom's mother rasped as she thrust the report into Tom's father's hand. "Tom's failed — 41%. What are we going to do?"

Tom's father held his hand up for quiet. Neither Tom's mother nor his brothers said a word while Harold studied the report.

After several minutes Harold spoke. "I don't see why you're so upset. Tom didn't fail as you interpret his report. He succeeded in doing what he wanted to do. He wanted to stay in grade 8 an extra year; he wanted to stay home an extra year; he wanted to be with his friends; he did what his friends wanted him to do. He wanted mediocrity, and he got it. Congratulations son! This calls for a celebration. Boys, here's some money. Go get the finest roast beef you can get and buy a cake. We'll celebrate. Tom deserves a feast. I'm proud of you, son."

A more miserable meal Tom had not eaten, a more miserable year that followed Tom had not lived up to then or since.

Tom forsook the macho style and left the road that led to mediocrity. He began to listen to his own common sense.

Tom is now a teacher.

THINK INDIAN

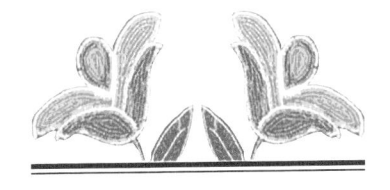

NO MAN BEGINS TO BE UNTIL

HE HAS RECEIVED THE VISION

BASIL H. JOHNSTON, O.ONT., LLD., B.A. ©

No Man Begins To Be Until

He Has Received The Vision

In rejecting the proposal of a missionary who had come to explain the Bible and the rewards and penalties for accepting or refusing the true religion, Red Jacket of the Seneca Nation, delivering a reply on behalf of the Iroquois there assembled said "… we shall see. If the Bible makes your people better, then we shall reconsider." What Red Jacket intended and meant in his answer was that in religion, as in other matters, belief and living out the beliefs were inseparable.

But in refuting the missionary's propositions, Red Jacket was not so much assessing the merit of the missionary's religion as he simply was affirming that a man's conduct ought to bear some relationship to his beliefs. According to him belief was no more important than the mode of abiding by those beliefs.

It is in terms of substance of belief and living out the beliefs that Indian religion must be regarded. That there is a body of beliefs respecting the origin, end, purpose and nature of being, the place and scope of man in creation, his duties to his God and fellow beings is established. What remains is to demonstrate that Indians tried to live out their beliefs in their daily lives accordingly as they understood them and as they saw fit. It is in this respect that Indian religion is to be assessed.

Central to Indian life was the vision. Of this event it was said that "no man begins to be until he has attained the vision." By the vision men gained an insight into themselves; through the vision men obtained direction and purpose, and in the vision men found their destinies. Thereafter they had to live out the vision; men had to be true to the vision.

Such was the force and place of vision in Indian life that from the moment they began to understand, infants were prepared for the vision. The preparation took two forms initially. First, because the vision was a gift, the infant was trained to receive. He was taught to dream and to be silent in the belief and knowledge that vision comes sometimes in dream and in silence or peace.

Through stories, the faculty for dreaming was fostered. At the same time, it was through stories that infants and youths learned about the origin and nature of things and learned what conduct was considered meritorious and what reprehensible. In infancy the stories told were simple, vivid and colourful, intended to produce good dreams in sleep. Later the stories were tragic and dramatic. Both kinds had as their ends the fostering of dreams and the teaching of the principles of good conduct.

Stories and songs, as they induced dreams, required silence and peace. It was believed that by listening, one would learn, and by thinking, one would understand. Listening was the art of commitment, a state of readiness to receive; peace was the great mystery to be sought within and without self. It was more than a negation; it was unity of heart and mind, a unity with a being and the spirit of the world.

Such was the way in which the soul-spirit was prepared; the physical frame was made ready by testings, numerous and severe. It too had to be rendered worthy for the reception of the sacred vision. For only when both moieties of a person were ready did the vision come.

For some, the vision came early; for others, later in life. In either case the central moment in life was attained. With its coming the person moved from the stage of youth to the state of adulthood; with the receipt of the vision a person's life assumed a new dimension in which his acts and his conduct took on a moral character. Thereafter, a person had to live out the vision; he had to be true to it.

The vision was a birth for man in the moral order. From the moment of the vision, "a man began to be."

In order to fulfill the vision he had to understand its substance and its implications insofar as he was capable. If necessary a person had to change in order to be true to his vision.

Difficult was the quest and not easy the attainment, and far more difficult was following the "path of life" indicated by the vision. That men sometimes failed to live up to the vision and digressed from the path was given cognizance on birch bark scrolls where the path of life was charted with branches leading from the main trail.

A man may lapse from his vision, but neither his acts nor his being were censured or construed as evil. No one knew his vision; he only was privy to it. Furthermore, transgressions were seldom perpetrated with malice, nor were they permanent in nature. To condemn, therefore, was to deny reform. The person who had received the vision went out each year and, in vigil, examined his own conduct, and if he found it tarnished, amended his life.

The vision was sacred and individual. It was a gift of Kitchi-Manitou, at least permitted by him, and it was of the spirit. If was for a person and not for anyone else. It was a gift personal, not to be shared with others. So strong was the conviction that men were enjoined "not to give their spirits; not to attempt to enter the spirit of another."

For those who had attained the vision, the vision became the principal source of morality. And as the vision was individual, morality was individual.

The second important source of morality was the Medaewaewin.

Originally established by medicine men and women learned in the use of herbs, roots and plants in the healing of illness and the relief of pain and for the fostering of greater knowledge, the medicine men and women came to realize that the purpose for the practice of medicine, the prolonging of human life was not sufficient to obtain the end. More was needed. Long life free from pain and sickness, they reasoned, was not so much to be procured from the prevention of sickness as it was to be secured from living a temperate life. All life was to be conducted in moderation.

By adding the element of good living to the curing arts, the medicine men and women were in fact giving substance to what is now accepted in medical practice that the physical well-being of an individual was related directly to his inner well-being. Sickness, they were implying, was the product of an inner turmoil.

What had to be fostered was inner peace. By incorporating this principle in their own lives and in the practice of their acts, the medicine men and women added a new dimension to themselves and to their profession.

From medicine men and women they became philosophers, accumulating knowledge about plants, but at the same time contemplating the quality of life and improving it. Just as the Mayans attempted to find a relationship between the good life and reward, and ill conduct and punishment, and endeavoured to regulate their daily lives by what they found, so the Anishinaubaek tried to govern their lives and conduct by establishing norms that would bring harmony between heard and mind whereby inner peace would be achieved. Inner peace obtained, a long life would ensue, it was believed.

From the time that the medicine men and women accepted the good life as part of their principle, the admission of new members into the society was predicated on knowledge of medicines and upon moral character. Thereafter, men and women of good will and good heart only were invited to membership in the Medaewaewin and, having been admitted, had to abide by the norms set up by the members.

Later, the vision was required of men. Women who, it seems, were not required to seek the vision, were invited on the strength of good character and knowledge.

In purpose and in scope the Medaewaewin became more than a medicine society for the perpetuation and dissemination of knowledge of plants; it became a society of thinkers who had to abide not only by the code of the Medaewaewin and the dictates of the vision, but by the customs and traditions of the tribe.

Men and women of solid moral fibre, and bound by vision though they might have been, were still subjected to a period of testing before full and final admission into the society. The candidates had to prove their knowledge and to demonstrate that they could abide by the codes of the society.

From the time of invitation it took a candidate four years of preparation and testing to pass through the four stages to fully accredited fellowship in the society. With the guidance of a tutor, the candidate mastered a body of knowledge respecting plants; the names, properties beneficial and noxious, uses, mixtures, solutions, and the songs and prayers that went with each. And each spring the candidate presented himself for testing to the assembly of the Medaewaewin.

THINK INDIAN

Before entering the Medaewaewin the initiate was required by custom and ritual to circumscribe the sacred lodge four times. Accompanied by his tutor, the candidate went around the lodge; four men dressed as bears symbolizing good went with him; four other bears representing evil that would prevent him fulfilling his duties as a member of the Medaewaewin, and encouraged at the same time by the guidance he would receive from those who would be his associates. And while the initiate's admission into the lodge on the fourth circuit may be regarded as the symbolic triumph of good over evil, the triumph may be construed only as temporary and transitory, never as final or permanent. Evil continues to exist in another realm. Evil has a place in life and may itself supersede good. Thus the candidate contemplates life as he goes around the sacred lodge.

And four times must the applicant present himself in four years to the accredited members of the Medaewaewin. Four times four times must he challenge the tests, and triumph over the obstacles and himself before he is deemed fit for full membership to sit beside the other members.

When the candidate is finally admitted as a fully qualified Medaewaewini, he too could sit and assess the suitability of other applicants who subsequently presented themselves. But his first duty was to live by the codes of the Medaewaewin.

For the new Medaewaewin member the struggle begins. Just as it was difficult for him to gain admission into the society, so was it difficult for him to regulate his life and conduct according to the ethics and norms of the society. In his pilgrimage around the lodge, the forces of evil that he had had to face and vanquish were represented by four bears. In his life as a Medaewaewini after admission, the temptations a man encountered were etched on sacred birch bark scrolls as short perilous paths branching out from the main trail. Surrender to temptations implies death. But that the divergent paths were connected to the main also implied that a man could return to the true way. Self examination was conducted at least annually to determine the tone of one's life.

To guide its members in the attainment of peace within and without themselves and to live in harmony with other beings the Medaewaewin set out the following code:

Thank Kitchi-Manitou for all things.

Honour the aged; and in honouring them, you honour life and wisdom.

Honour life in all its forms, and your own will be sustained.

Honour women; in honouring them, you honour life giving.

Honour parents; in honouring them, you honour the gift of love.

Honour kindness; by honouring kindness, you will be kind.

Honour peace; by honouring peace, you will be peaceful.

Honour courage; by honouring courage, you will be courageous.

Honour promises; by living up to your promises, you will be true to self.

Be true to the Medaewaewin; by fidelity to the Medaewaewin, you will find truth.

Be moderate in all things; listen, watch, think and your deeds will be prudent.

Such then were the principles adopted by the Medaewaewin for the guidance of its members in attaining peace and development of character. Simple the norms were, yet encompassing and noble.

For all, from youth to old age, whether endowed with vision or enshrined in the Medaewaewin, there were rituals and ceremonies exercised from time immemorial to be observed.

Each morning, with the rise of the sun the first person rising from his pallet went outside the lodge and, facing the east, said a prayer of thanks to the sun:

I thank you, Kitchi-Manitou
For your light
I thank you
For new life
I begin life anew
Fresh and unburdened.

Likewise at night, as the sun sank over the western rim a person faced west, man's last destination, and rendered a prayer of thanks:

THINK INDIAN

I thank you, Kitchi-Manitou
For the gifts
For the good
Of the day passed.

Twice daily were prayers said in every lodge, prayers of gratitude to Kitchi-Manitou.

Then there were prayers said by hunters upon killing game. There were no standard prayers, but each man intoned his own prayer in his own fashion.

Most of the prayers uttered were simple and expressed regret for the taking of life, or gratitude to Kitchi-Manitou for providing the game. A hunter might say "Forgive me, my need was greater than yours," or "Forgive me, I did not kill you in anger."

A woman planting a seed also said a prayer to one of the manitous giving life, birth and growth, to the seed itself, to rain, to the sun, or to the earth, asking for abundance.

At harvest time the harvesters tendered thanks to Kitchi-Manitou for his generosity.

Along with individual private prayers of thanks there were public and communal ceremonies of thanks combining prayer, song and dance. In the autumn there was a Thanksgiving festival in thanksgiving to Kitchi-Manitou for survival, for preserving the lives of men, women and children during the winter.

The prayers said were expressions of the heart and even open declarations of debts and obligations owed. Often they were plain petitions for wisdom and acknowledgements of man's dependence upon game placed in a fortuitous place by Kitchi-Manitou.

Prayers, naked and alone, mean little. Prayers express only an attitude. Rather it is deed that gives force and meaning to belief and attitude. And with respect to life the Anishinaubaek performed deed.

In killing game, all the flesh was eaten and all the bones used. There was no waste. It was believed that it was in this way that life was respected. Furthermore, a female animal with young was spared. Nor were all beaver in a lodge or lake killed. Only what was needed was taken. A male and female were always left to propagate. Men tried to avoid desecration.

Similarly, plants were honoured. Plants used for food or medicine were picked only when fully grown and had lived out their full term of life and had fulfilled their other purposes. If only a part of a plant was required, then only that portion that was needed was picked. Were the entire plant to be used, tobacco was offered or another seed placed in the vacuum.

And during the mixing of plants and roots and powders in the manufacture of medicines, a prayer was said, and only as much as was needed was made.

Thus were plants honoured and their beings conserved.

There were death songs chanted by those who faced death:

> *I do not fear death.*
> *My time has come.*
> *I will walk the Path of Souls.*
> *To the Land of Souls.*
>
> *To the Land of Peace.*

The dead were placed on scaffolds with their feet pointing to the west, the direction of the Path of Souls. By leaving the body exposed and free, the soul-spirit was enabled in its own time to take leave of its earthly frame. After death there was a period of mourning lasting for a year. Only by the Feast of the Dead held on the anniversary of the dead was the mourner released from the period of mourning.

Such were the prayers, individual and public, celebrations that were practiced daily and annually by the Anishinaubaek.

There were no priests, only medicine men and women; only the aged who led the ceremonies; all took part. There were no churches; prayer and celebration took place in the forest, meadow and stream as occasion demanded the utterance and offering of prayer. There were no written codes of law and ethics binding men and women under pain of punishment to perform; custom and individual conscience dictated what was to be done. Yet the Anishinaubaek were religious.

In the ceremonies there were the four orders represented: the rock, the fire, the air and the water. There were four parts to each ceremony: the purification, the preparation, the offering and, finally, the festival in which all took part in the dancing or thanksgiving. All life and being were honoured.

The Anishinaubaek were religious in belief and in attitude, as well as in deed.

THINK INDIAN

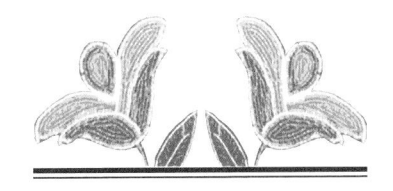

SKILLS OR UNDERSTANDING

KNOWLEDGE OR WISDOM

BASIL H. JOHNSTON, O.ONT., LLD., B.A. ©

Skills or Understanding

Knowledge or Wisdom

Few peoples have been studied more and understood less than are the Native peoples of the Americas. For all the study and research conducted; for all the books and methodologies used; and for all the grants expended, few peoples or subjects have been appreciated less. The fault may be imputed in part to the philosophy of education, in part to the quality of materials, and in part to methodology.

If the Native peoples and their heritage are to be understood, it is their beliefs, understandings, insights, ideals, values, ethics and attitudes that must be studied and, not as at present, their kinship systems, structures of their organizations, or forms of their religions.

And there is no better way of gaining that insight than by study of Native ceremonies, songs, dances and stories, whether stories are considered as legend, fable or myth. For it is in ceremony, song and dance that the sum total of what Native people believe about life, being, existence and relationships is symbolically expressed, as it is in story that their fundamental understandings, insights and attitudes toward life and human conduct in all its forms are inscribed.

If, therefore, Native peoples and their cultures are to be understood and better appreciated, and if the end of education be to foster a love of truth and a quest for wisdom, to uphold law and tradition and at the same time preserve the inviolability of the individual, and to encourage freedom in the form of personal growth while instilling a sense of duty toward others, then I state with confidence that Native Indian stories, by their nature and character, would confer a deeper understanding and wider appreciation of Native life and cultural than through a study of technologies, techniques or kinship systems.

That Native stories, because of their creative and imaginative patterns, would foster imagination and creativity much more forcefully than a study of structures and manners.

That Native stories, based upon a knowledge of human nature and character, and harbouring great themes, could foster another understanding of the moral order and inspire a quest for truth and wisdom.

That the sooner Native stories are resurrected from the realm of antiquity and curiosity and given recognition for what they represent, the better it will be for teachers, students, Natives, and the whole fabric of Native Studies.

For the good and good will intended by the Departments of Education of this country in permitting greater latitude to schools in offering courses will not be attained unless the philosophy of education is reviewed and amended. Certainly revisions of Departments of Education, regulations respecting curriculae have not nurtured improvements in Native Studies courses. That there are exceptions does not rebut the general allegation as to the sad state of affairs.

What is occurring in principle had long ago been observed by the Native peoples and embodied in the story of The Man, The Snake, and The Fox, "that man, in seeking good, may sometimes confer evil."

The good, better understanding of the Native peoples and their cultures is the aspiration of Native peoples themselves and the objective of education. The evil consists in aversion, often pity for, and a misconceived notion of what constitutes merit in Indian life. Too often the attitude that Indian life is devoid of depth or validity has been fostered by insufficient knowledge, unimaginative preparation, uninspired pedagogy and deficient books.

But what has conferred the greatest disservice to Native Studies programs, and to many others for that matter, has been the influence of technology. Teachers and educators, dazzled and overwhelmed by the electronic age and miracles of technology, have repudiated humanism. In its place they have substituted the study of method, structure and progress, and embraced machinery in the classroom.

Within this framework Native Studies courses consist of studies of transportation in all its forms: snowshoeing, canoeing and horsemanship; examination of varieties of dwellings: long houses, teepees and lodges; analysis of

THINK INDIAN

food preparation: boiling, baking, roasting and drying; research into clothing as to pattern, design and beadwork. At higher levels in education the emphasis is on problems, structures and forms. Hardly, I submit, inspiring or conferring understanding of the staff of life.

From bottom to top the spectre and mood and tone of technology has insinuated itself into education. Instead of the pursuit of truth and wisdom, the development of skills is deliberately encouraged; instead of the growth of character, the study personality is engendered; instead of giving to old tradition new form, its destruction is urged. It is the means rather than the end that is primal. In this atmosphere there is no vision, little or no provision for the encouragement for man's inner growth, when the need is greatest.

It is not uncommon for students to anticipate a course on one of the tribes of North America. But after devoting five weeks in the construction of a model teepee in the classroom for display on Parent-Teachers Open House night, youngsters have been known to express their disenchantment with "I'm sick of Indians." To the Native peoples such a response is disappointing but not surprising. Had the motive and the approach for the project been different, perhaps the results might have been happier.

Instancy is one of the characteristics of the electronic and technological age. Speed, skim, and complete in the shortest time possible. Courses conducted in computer style are shallow. In this climate there is no time for depth. As a consequence, great civilizations such as that of the Maya, Aztec and Inca have been shabbily treated. The efforts have not been comparable to the greatness that these cultures represent and deserve.

In five weeks the histories of the Aztecs and the Incas have been studied in terms of human sacrifice, siestas, food, clothing and shelter. Seldom, if ever, is the essence of the civilization explored. What is disturbing is not so much that students were introduced to the unpleasant and even trifling aspects of a culture, but that so much of substance and merit has been neglected. For this tragedy, the spirit of technology and poor preparation, and not good books is to be blamed.

Secondary school courses, with all their extravagant equipment, degreed teachers, endless resources, do little better. Admittedly, there is broader scope and depth to courses. Native speakers are invited to expound and explain, films are shown to generate interest, seminars are conducted to inspire communication, and resource kits hastily and haphazardly assembled by academics serve as authorities. Yet for all these advantages, there is precious little real understanding.

After a course in Indian studies students can command statistics on welfare, criminality and employment. They may know how to undertake research. They may acquire sympathy and commiseration for the Natives. But what other result can be expected from quasi-sociological and mathematical approaches to the study of human beings. A knowledge of facts and methods takes precedence over the pursuit of wisdom.

Nor, it is submitted, is the situation in our universities and colleges much better. The content and approach to courses reflect popular demand and represent a surrender to the mechanistic and materialistic aspects of current values and interpretations of human life. By yielding to popular pressure and substituting process for substance, universities have abdicated from their responsibilities whereby they have lost some of their credibility.

In some of the Native Studies courses themes such as cultural conflict, social structure, integration, and a search for identity are based to a large extent on current interest and ultimately on process and not on what is lasting and substantial. With the possible exception of Indians and the Law, the study of ideals, principles, feelings and understandings do not form an essential part of a course. Following the completion of a course, the student still does not know what constitutes an Indian or Native culture. The Indian remains an abstract.

At no point in the educational process and system has the Native and his thoughts and feelings about those matters that have concerned mankind been studied. As a result, the Native and his legacy remain mysterious; his ways, manners and customs are well known, his soul and spirit remain untouched. To some he is a noble savage, to others he remains a simple savage.

Since the anticipated good in Native education has not been achieved, the time has come for the authorities in education to review the philosophy of education which determines the pattern and content of education, and ultimately the destiny of the nation.

Teachers too must reassess their functions in education. Either they are agents of technology or they are advocates of the quest for wisdom. If society espouses wisdom as the end of education, and if society is to suppose that its teachers have as their purpose the search for truth and ultimately the quest for wisdom, then teachers can do no better than by restoring the story to its rightful place in education.

Assignments, exercises, projects can confer skills and knowledge only the story can, because it embodies wisdom, imparts wisdom.

Indian stories ought to be an integral part of the educational process without prejudice to methodology or technique. Its recommended adoption is not intended to displace audio-visual equipment but to complement it by infusing into the process insights, interest and the spirit and mood of wisdom.

But storytelling is a difficult art. The meanings of each story must be understood in all aspects, levels and implications. But unless the teacher understands the stories, how is the student to comprehend? Unless the teacher tells the stories, how is the student to know that there is more to Native Indian culture than moccasins, beads and birch bark baskets? Unless the teacher tells the stories, how are students to begin contemplating profound matters such as:

> *No Man Begins To Be, Until He Has Received His Vision*
>
> *To Own Is To Be Owned*
>
> *I Am The First Of Men; The Last Of Men*
>
> *A Man Intending Good May Also Inflict Evil*
>
> *Seek The Truth; Live It Out*
>
> *Do Not Give Too Freely Of Your Spirit*
>
> *One Act Of Courage Does Not Make Courage*
>
> *Silence Is A Mystery*

To understand the meanings of stories is difficult. It requires effort. And to admit that the insights of other people have merit and validity needs an open mind.

In recommending the restoration of stories and particularly the institution of Native stories into Native Studies and courses to their proper sphere in education and instruction I mean the narrated story. This is not to disparage good reading. There are, I suppose, circumstances in which stories may, with profit, be read to an audience. But narration, well done, is always to be preferred.

Reading has too many limitations. Stories that have been written down are too often prescribed for a specific audience, a grade level. Moreover, the style is intended for readers and not for listeners. And far too frequently reading is badly conceived and poorly done.

Stories in general, and Indian stories specifically, ought not to be prescribed as to content, place, time and audience. By virtue of the depth and scope of their themes stories deserve to be told and perpetuated. As men wish to grow in wisdom they are entitled to share in the legacy of wisdom embodied in stories.

Narration has greater scope. On the premise that stories are meant for all generations and for every shade of understanding, need and taste, narrators are free to recount stories according to their own natural style for the understanding of their audience. They are at liberty to alter details such as names, times, places, characters and order. What is paramount is the exposition of theme and lessons.

Narration has another advantage. The narrator can create moods, modify, suspend, to even sustain them. Both narrator and audience are conjoined in mood, spirit and feeling. For scope, reading cannot match pure narration.

There is one other principle in storytelling that runs in the Indian story, and for all stories. While it is true that some stories are of such depth as to require interpretation for understanding, it is often better to allow the listener to draw his own inferences. To induce the listener to think is the essence of the art of teaching, inspiration. And to allow the listener to draw his own conclusions is the highest form of respect for his intellectual capacity and for his integrity. No greater disservice can be perpetuated upon a person that to deny him self growth than by over-teaching or instantaneous interpretation. Tell the story and allow the listener to understand according to his own capacity. Time and ability will enable him to make deductions.

Indian legends need time for understanding; they are intended to be understood in many ways.

If the restoration of the real aims of education rests on change in the philosophy of education, then the Departments of Education in this country must renounce the philosophy that encourages only the acquisition of skills and knowledge; they must adopt another philosophy that engenders humanism and understanding. For it is only by return to the fundamental principles of education that understanding and appreciation of the Native peoples and their heritage will be gained. Only within a different framework will stories again fulfill their noble purposes.

And if narration is to be restored as an art and supersede films and tape recorders, then the Departments of Education must sponsor, and the universities of this land conduct courses that will teach the fundamentals of storytelling.

And if Native stories are to be understood, then Native storytellers must not only restore them to their own fabric of life, but assist in the understanding of the stories.

The Royal Ontario Museum, because it is committed to and perpetuates "wisdom through the ages," can assist teachers in the interpretation of stories, and offer understandings not normally available to educators.

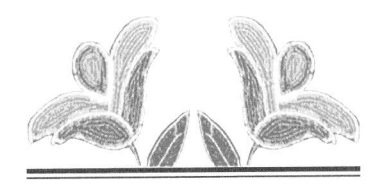

WHERE IS THE FLOUR?

BASIL H. JOHNSTON, O.ONT., LLD., B.A. ©

THINK INDIAN

Where Is The Flour?

In the 30s and 40s most Western movie fans could tell anyone who cared to ask who Tonto was, although they may not have known that Tonto was really Jay Smith of Ohsweken, Ontario, otherwise known as Jay Silverheels. But Mr. Jay Silverheels wasn't the only Indian in Hollywood. Jim Thorpe, once the best athlete in the Western world, was there, along with a band of nameless Indians from various tribes across North America. Among this band of moving picture Indians was Norman Peter Joshua Jones of Cape Croker, whose name was included in the film credits but rolled by so quickly that no one noticed.

Even if Norman Peter Joshua Jones had been a household name in the world outside the reservation, the Chippewas wouldn't have given a poop.

Of course, when "Josh" as he was known at Cape Croker came home after a few years of absence, word spread that he had been in Hollywood, California. People, especially the young people of the movie generation, asked Josh if he'd ever seen Tom Mix, Gene Autry, Ken Maynard, Hoot Gibson or Johnny Mack Brown.

"Yes! In fact, I made some movies with them!" Josh drawled.

"You did?" the young asked in doubtful reverence; they wanted to believe Josh but held back, not wanting to be taken in. Josh, a chip off the old block, C.K. Jones Sr., might have inherited the old man's gift of exaggeration.

Instead of asking Josh what movies he'd acted in or for his autograph that cultured people are in the habit of asking, the Cape Croker Chippewa wanted to know how Josh found his way to California.

"Waaal, I tell … you …" he drawled. "It was like this. Dad sent me to Johnston's store to get five pounds of flour. Johnston didn't have any so I kept on going to Purple Valley. Wasn't any flour there either. And knowing what dad was like, I didn't dare go home empty handed. I kept on walking until I got to Wiarton. When I got to town I couldn't for the life of me remember what dad had sent me to town for, so I just kept on going. Eventually I'd remember. Along the way I earned my room and board by doing odd jobs as a carpenter's helper. Kept on movin' until I couldn't go any further. Ran out o' land; just water as far as I could see.

I didn't know where I was so I asked some folks I met to tell me what town I was in and what lake was in front of my way.

'You're in Hollywood,' they said, 'and that there body of water is the Pacific Ocean.'

I took a long look at that ocean; couldn't see the other side. It was like trying to look to the far side of Georgian Bay.

By now I was next to being broke. I had to find me a job in order to eat and sleep. There were times when I longed for the good old days when a man could travel, eat and sleep without payin' a cent for his meals or for a patch of ground to sleep on. Wishful thinkin' that, but them days are gone. Waaal! Those same folks who told me that I was in Hollywood let me know that there was an outfit called Universal International that was looking for carpenters to build 'sets'. What sets were I didn't know, but I was too hungry to let not knowing what 'sets' were to hold me back from applying for a job.

Along the way from the reservation I learned that a man can't be too backward in order to get ahead. Just one of the things that I learned from the White folks that I worked for and with. So when the foreman asked me if I could handle tools I spread the lark thick … told the man that I could handle any kind of saw: cross-cut, Swede, Norwegian; that I played with nothin' but axes and rulers even when I was a toddler. Got hired and started next day. And making 'sets' is what I did for the next few years.

It was around this time that Hollywood got interested in Indians for their Western movies. Real Indians would give Western movies authenticity and save the studios a pile of money. Universal International, the outfit that I worked for, got on the band wagon-train as well.

As a real genuine Indian on Universal International payroll, my stock with the studio shot up a few percentage points. I was worth something. I knew something that the White folks didn't know; the Chippewa language, customs, traditions, dress and the way that Indians look at things. I became an unofficial consultant, for which I was given parts as an extra in Cowboys and Indian movies. That's how I came to know Tom Mix and Jim Thorpe."

"Josh! How come you never got famous like Tonto?"

Josh considered that question some moments before replying. "Waaal" he picked up his drawl where he'd left off. "I guess it was because I always played minor roles ... part of a gang of whooping, hollering Indians, killing and getting killed. Can't get famous getting killed. There were times when I wished I was famous; my name up there in big, black block letters, bright little lights dancing around it. But I don't think that I was cut out for that sort of thing. Being famous is a heavy pack to carry around. I could never own myself to do what I would like to do. Besides, fame don't sit too well with Indians. Instead of being proud of their brothers and sisters for accomplishing something, Indians knock him down and say 'Thinks he's pretty good, him. But he's no better than nobody else; needs to be reminded where he belongs' ... neighbours here at home would've belted me for being famous and wouldn't speak to me."

"Well then, how come that Tonto got a leading role and got famous?"

"I don't want to take anything from Tonto, but he didn't really play a leading role. It was the Lone Ranger who was the star. He got all the glory. Tonto was more like a chore boy, making camp, building fires, making tea and cleaning up. Big roles weren't meant for Indians, Blacks, Hindus or Asiatics; big roles were meant for White folks."

"Why's that, Josh?"

"Waaal, I tell you how I see it. White folks like to think of themselves and champions. They want to rescue and save someone. They have to do that; they can't lose. They are more holy than anybody else, so they gotta convert the pagans; they're more law-abiding that anybody else, so they gotta punish the wrong-doers. Nobody can compare to them.

But every once in a while someone from another race shows them up in real life. For such a thing to happen is a hard biscuit for the White folks to swallow. That sort of thing is not supposed to happen, and if it happens it's an accident or the result of cheating. When our brother Jim Thorpe beat all the best athletes that the White folks brought together in the 1911 Olympics, the White folks couldn't believe that an Indian could be better than the best that the White folks sent to Helsinki in Finland. They wouldn't believe than an Indian outran, outjumped, outleaped, outhurled White athletes honestly and fairly. That Indian must have cheated.

And of course the White folks who didn't do that sort of thing dug in some skeletons in Jim Thorpe's back yard. The horror of horrors, that Indian had received a few filthy dollars for playing baseball for the New York Giants. Imagine, getting a few bucks for hitting and catching a baseball made Jim faster, stronger, and gave him more endurance than anyone else. That conniving Indian cheated; the only way he could beat a White man. So the purists took the medals away from Jim Thorpe and gave them to the White athletes who came in second. The White people have to win."

"Why's that, Josh?"

"That's hard to say. They're so hard to figure out. So many good people among them. Many more than the bad apples, but it's the bad apples that create the stink. Ever since I started working with the White folks I've been trying to figure them out.

I kind of suspect that the White folks aren't as cock-sure about their superiority as they'd like to be. They have to keep reminding themselves that no one can match them.

And there's no better forum for improving one's image than a motion picture camera. Just like a mirror. Movies can make people look better than they really are, or worse. Take your pick. Makeup artists can brush out blackheads and pimples just as easily as they can dab them on. Brush out what mars the image; show the good side. Show what the people want to see about themselves. Movie screens projected a handsome image, a beautiful face with a dulcet voice that told the viewer 'You are the fairest, justest, kindest, truest, smartest, noblest, chastest, honestest, gentlest folks in the entire kingdom.'

Movies are not unlike mirrors, capable of showing only faces, bodies and settings, not the soul or spirit of a person or the vibrancy of the earth. If cameras and mirrors could see beneath surfaces and into the inner being of a person, they might well show what the viewer didn't expect or want to see or hear. Instead of answering 'You are the fairest or them all' as the mirror said to the queen, the mirror might reply 'you are a thin-skinned, overbearing, double-dealing, moralizing, righteous, avaricious, selfish old hag.'

Hearing such an answer would not send spasms of shame into the viewer or induce him to beat his chest in repentance and promise reform. No, he wouldn't do such a thing. Instead, he'd pitch a rock at the screen and curse the producers and the director for distorting reality.

Such a reaction is to be expected. People, no matter what race, like to see themselves s decent human beings, as they should be. Few see themselves as they really are; they are afraid that they might not be as good as they think they are. They are afraid that they might buckle when the crunch comes.

Deep down they want to be good and they want to show and tell the world that they are good guys. But it isn't easy to convince the descendants of slaves that their ancestors' masters were benevolent and that the descendants of masters shouldn't be held accountable for the misdeeds of their ancestors. The landless who were stripped of their lands and their freedoms are not about to nod in agreement that the pirates who took their lands were honourable human beings. The offspring of the victims of war, persecution, occupation, injustice, discrimination, false imprisonment are not about to grant that the offenders were men of good will. With so much guilt, it's difficult to show good will.

Instead of apologizing or making amends to doubtful victims, the offenders want to unload the guilt. They want to be told that they are good guys; they have a pathological need to be looked up to. But the White folks can't shrug off their guilt so long as their victims are alive.

It wasn't until motion pictures were developed that the White folks found a way of unloading some of their guilt. They created Hollywood. There in the world of make believe, movie makers and makeup artists transformed scullery maids into queens, queens into hags; converted villains into upright men, upright men into villains. They made bad look good, good look bad. There was evil to be stamped out, good to be nourished. It was through motion pictures and movies that the White folks projected the image of themselves that they wanted the world to see; hid or passed over what was offensive to the shoulders of others.

Until recently, White actors played the leading roles in most pictures, chasing bad guys and bringing them to justice, cleaning up neighbourhoods and making it safe for White folks. Indians, Blacks, Asiatics were extras; they played bad guys who perpetrated crimes and misdemeanours for which they were brought to trial and locked up or cut down in a hail of gunfire. They deserved what they got in the world of make believe and in reality. This shifting of blame reduced the weight of guilt that the White folks had been carrying around while it increased the guilt of the other races.

Our role as extras was to act as bad guys in order to make the White folks look good. We had no choice. The White folks owned the studios, wrote the scripts and published books from which the screen plays were adapted. They were the ones who assigned us bad guy roles.

But it didn't matter much. The White folks needed to look good much more than we did. None of us complained because the studio paid us a pretty good wage for being bad guys. I skulked, lied, stole, raided, burned wagon trains, scalped prisoners, kidnapped women and children, fell off horses, ran away, whooped and groaned, got hurt and died quite a few times. Became an expert at dying; easiest thing to do.

Good as we were, we Indians could never get top billing. If someone had to portray a chief or a famous Indian, it had to be a White man, some like Jeff Chandler.

I had to train people like that. But I didn't remain as Indian coach for too long. Within a few years the bigwigs brought in anthropologists from universities and museums to the sets and sites to show us how to be real Indians.

To be displaced by smart guys didn't matter much to us Indians because it didn't change anything. We were Indians, bad guys who didn't know much. Our role in the world of make believe and in the working world was to boost the White folks' image and morale.

While I was in Hollywood I kept asking myself 'What am I doing here building false fronts, living a false life?'

I would have gone home earlier except that I met Una, a seamstress at the studio. Couldn't keep my mind off that woman after I seen her. Turned out that Una couldn't keep me out of her mind either. And to settle our feelings, we got married. Wonderful institution, marriage; just the thing to heal the affliction of love. Became a producer then!"

Josh paused to let this bit of information sink in.

"You were a producer?"

"Yes ... me and Una produced Shirley, Jean, Normie Ann, Joan, Bob, Bill, Howard, Norman ... but even after I got married I kept thinking about home and dad. Then I remembered I was supposed to get five pounds of flour. I could image the old man, must be about 85 now, sitting there on a chair on the porch by the doorway looking across the harbour and down the road. Got more lonesome as the years limped along.

I told Una that I was thinking of going home to my reservation in Canada.

I bought a truck, packed all our belongings and electrical appliances: stove, fridge and Una's electric sewing machine into the truck and we rumbled all the way across the continent. Just before we set out I told Una to remind me to get flour when we got to Wiarton.

"Took 8 days to make that trek from Hollywood to Cape Croker."

"You got the flour that I sent you to the store for?" was the first thing that dad said when I got out of my truck with my wife and our children.

"Sorry I took so long dad" I apologized.

THINK INDIAN

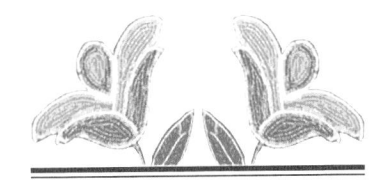

IS THERE A PLACE FOR ME ON THIS BLANKET?

(THE PLACE OF THE INDIAN IN THE MULTI-CULTURAL FABRIC OF CANADA)

BASIL H. JOHNSTON, O.ONT., LLD., B.A.©

THINK INDIAN

Is There A Place For Me On This Blanket?

(The Place of the Indian in the Multi-cultural Fabric of Canada)

This nation, so full of promise, is divided in spirit and impaired in heart. So long as its peoples are in discord over religion, politics, race, economics, so long will the nation be weak. So long as one part countenances and another portion suffers poverty and injustice, so long will the nation be discontent. In this state the nation's spirit remains unformed, stunted, incapable of fulfilling its noble promise.

Yet the differences that divide and enfeeble may also unit and buttress, fortify. Such is the character and the nature of diversity. In matters cultural, the diversity in Canada may enrich the nation, confer a unique identity, and enhance the conduct of national affairs. It may even bring prosperity where there is poverty, and heal wounds through justice and good will. Men may then be of different minds but of one heart.

The fulfillment of this promise will depend upon those who possess the power. The English and the French-speaking may allow their differences to overwhelm the needs of the nation. They may even regard their legacies and affairs as superseding those of others. By so doing they can destroy this nation. But by foregoing their controversies the English and the French can foster growth and trust.

Peoples whose origin is neither English nor French have a stake in this nation and a claim in the conduct of its affairs. As members of this nation they are entitled to share not only in its produce and bounty, but also in the determination of its future course and character. They cannot be excluded because they are few; they ought not to be denied because they have not the power. Weak and strong are brothers in this community. All are entitled to a portion of the Blanket.

Fortunately the capacity and talents of people and races are not prescribed by numbers. While it may be true of economics and politics that there ought to be some proportion between consumption and production, representation and population, no such proportion in other spheres exists or is required between merit and numbers. The few have as much to give as the many; the few have as much talent and service to render in guiding the destiny of this nation.

What's true of other minorities is true of Indians.

You are familiar with the material contributions of the Native people of this continent, how they assisted your forefathers, how they served the nation in two great wars, and how they shared their foods with the peoples of the world.

In the past too much heed has been paid to the material aspects of the cultural legacies of Indians, too little to the essence. For want of appreciation, the intellectual culture mouldered and wasted away. But the manufacture of artifacts, or performance of dances form but one aspect of men's endeavours.

There is another dimension to Indian life, another side that makes up the heart, the soul, the character and the identity of the Indian people.

As Indian people engaged in practical matters, they sought to understand life. And, according to how they saw it, attempted to regulate their modes of living and existing. In so doing, they left a wealth of views and a variety of attitudes, a richness in values, a breadth of insights into life and living. Herein lies the essence and substance of the Indian heart and soul; herein reposes the real attainment and the merit of the Indians.

In a short paper I can do no better than to offer a sketch of the depth and scope of Native thought. If you find merit and accept the Indian approach to certain matters, we are honoured. If your adoption enhances your mode and improves our conditions, we are gratified. But hope for more is presumptuous.

Are you to reject, as I expect, that the Indian approach to life is a valid one, or that it has wider application than you can admit, or that it still has meaning and force for the Native peoples. As it has sustained their dignity in the past, it can continue to do so in the future. The very least that can be expected is for the Native people to be allowed to conduct their affairs in the traditional manner.

THINK INDIAN

Were you to allow the coming of Indian values and modes into your own culture, hearts would begin to come together, the Canadian spirit would then grow larger and begin to take on new forms and expressions. Much good would ensue.

Our understanding of certain common fundamental matters would be increased. We would discover, in our differences and similarities, merit and worth and begin to compose our mistrust and our enmities that divide our hearts and poison our minds.

Hearts becoming one, minds may still entertain very different opinions; hearts becoming united in purpose, the character and quality of the spirit of the nation would grow and prosper.

Just as the heart and mind may be enriched by Native attitudes and values, so too the mode of doing certain things may be enriched.

From his conception of man's composition and nature the Indian framed his values, habits and principles that governed his relationship with the physical world, his family, his neighbours and his community.

The Indians had a special reverence for the land and its harvest. Such esteem may be espoused for the preservation of animal-kind and the conservation of our dwindling resources.

The spirit that fostered reverence for the land also formulated the notion that land ownership resided in all men, not in just the one or the few; not only in the present generation, but also the next; and that the bounty of the earth existed for all men. Accordingly, men were considered to be trustees of the land and its produce. As such, they were to respect the rights of future generations, and ensure that the needy received their just share of the earth's proceeds. Given fresh expression in a practical way, such an approach could mitigate hardships and overcome resentments today.

Indians regarded the earth as primal, as a mother; themselves as children of the earth, brothers in life. Insofar as they shared the same needs and a similar nature, endured similar hardships, all were entitled to food, clothing, education, health care, and shelter. These constituted men's basic rights; other matters were secondary, privileges.

Birth conferred rights, tradition gave place and scope. Reason and tradition protected, guided and limited; conferred duties. All men were bound to enlarge their inner beings, and to look after the weak and poor. Leaders had no authority or power; they received support only as long as they served the poor and secured the safety of the community.

Leaders were, moreover, to redress wrongs. And the most equitable way of mending harms, they came to realize, was not by punishing the wrong-doer, but by compensating the victim. But the adjustment of wrongs was always difficult, and depended upon wisdom and generosity of spirit.

But the real onus for instilling a sense of law and order in the young rested upon the wise; the responsibility for harms done upon the family. Through stories, the young learned principles; in the vision they obtained understanding and inspiration and guidance in living out principles.

As his fellow man gave him wisdom, the individual returned the gift in the form of service for his fellow man. The end for both was growth and strength in spirit.

What the individual is to his community an ethnic group is to the nation. The nation, allowing the ethnic group scope for growth, will in turn receive immeasurable benefits. The nations refusing will constrict and choke upon its denials.

There is in our country much division that has arrested growth. There is likewise, in the talents and energies of its various peoples, abundant powers to heal and he powers to grow. This is the promise that needs fulfillment. What is needed is an "openness of heart" to move these powers and to bring strength and resolve and purpose to the nation.

As members of this nation endowed with certain talents and energies, as signatories to treaties vested with certain rights.

As members of this nation with roots embedded from time immemorial.

As members of this nation wishing to retain their identities.

As members of this nation with a share in the present and the future.

THINK INDIAN

Indians claim, demand and deserve a place by the side of their compatriots in shaping the destiny of this nation. They claim a place as a matter of right; they demand a place as a matter of service; they deserve a place as men need to grow in spirit and dignity.

THINK INDIAN

Other Great Kegedonce Press Titles

The Colour of Dried Bones, by Lesley Bellaeu
isbn: 978-0-9784998-0-8 (paper)

Without Reservation: Indigenous Erotica
edited by Kateri Akiwenzie-Damm
isbn: 0-9731396-2-5 (paper)
isbn 13: 978-0-9731936-2-4

Steepy Mountain love poetry, by Joanne Arnott
isbn: 0-9731396-3-3 (paper)
isbn 13: 978-0-9731396-3-1

Skins: Contemporary Indigenous Writing
edited by Kateri Akiwenzie-Damm & Josie Douglas
isbn: 0-9697120-6-5 (paper)
isbn 13: 978-0-9697120-6-0

Honour Earth Mother: Mino-audjaudauh Mizzu-kummik Quae
by Basil Johnston
isbn: 0-9731396-1-7 (paper)
isbn 13: 978-0-9731396-1-7

Spirit Horses, by Al Hunter
featuring artwork by Leo Yerxa
isbn: 0-9697120-8-1 (paper)
isbn 13: 978-0-9697120-8-4

The Glass Lodge, by John McDonald
isbn: 0-9731396-4-1 (paper)
isbn 13: 978-0-9731396-4-8

my heart is a stray bullet, by Kateri Akiwenzie-Damm
isbn: 0-9697120-9-x (paper)
isbn 13: 978-0-969-7120-9-1

The Long Dance, by David A. Groulx
isbn: 0-9697120-5-7 (paper)
isbn 13: 978-0-9697120-5-3

looking into the eyes of my forgotten dreams, by Joseph A. Dandurand
isbn: 0-9697120-4-9 (paper)
isbn 13: 978-0-969-7120-4-6

The Gift of the Stars, by Basil Johnston
isbn: 978-0-9784998-6-0

Under god's pale bones, by David A. Groulx
isbn: 978-0-9784998-8-4

W'Daub Awae: Speaking True, A Kegedonce Press Anthology
edited by Dr. Warren Cariou
isbn: 978-0-9784998-5-3

Borderlines & Bloodlines, by Gloria Alvernaz-Mulcahy
isbn: 978-0-9784998-4-6

Love Medicine and One Song, by Gregory Scofield
isbn 13: 978-0-9784998-2-2

Kynship, Book One, by Daniel Heath Justice
isbn: 09731396-6-8 (paper)
isbn 13: 978-0-9731396-6-2

Wyrwood, Book Two, by Daniel Heath Justice
isbn: 0-9731396-7-6 (paper)
isbn 13: 978-0-9731396-7-9

Dreyd, Book Three, by Daniel Heath Justice
isbn: 0-9731396-5-x (paper)
isbn 13: 978-0-9731396-5-5

Stone the Crow, A Book of Poems, by Chris Bose
isbn: 978-0-9784998-3-9

The Recklessness of Love,
Bawajiganan gaye Ni-maanedam (Dreams and Regrets)
by Al Hunter
isbn: 13: 978-0-9784998-1-5

that tongued belonging, by Marilyn Dumont
isbn: 978-0-9731396-9-3 (paper)

Angel Wing Splash Pattern, by Richard Van Camp
isbn: 0-9731396-0-9 (paper)
isbn 13: 978-0-9731396-0-0